JEWISH AMERICA

JEWISH AMERICA

SEYMOUR KURTZ

McGRAW-HILL BOOK COMPANY

New York   St. Louis   San Francisco
Bogotá   Guatemala   Hamburg   Lisbon
Madrid   Mexico   Montreal   Panama   Paris
San Juan   São Paulo   Tokyo   Toronto

1 2 3 4 5 6 7 8 9 HAL HAL 8 7 6 5

ISBN 0-07-035655-6

LIBRARY OF CONGRESS CATALOGING IN PUBLICATION DATA

Kurtz, Seymour.
　Jewish America.
　　1. Jews—United States—History.　2. United States—
Ethnic relations.　I. Title.
E184.J5K88　1985　　　973'.04924　　　　84–10065
ISBN 0–07–035655–6

Book design by Roberta Rezk

FOR MATTHEW AND ANYA

Contents

Acknowledgments

THERE WERE MANY who helped in the making of this essay on the history and living spirit of a fascinating and complex people, the American Jews. Worthy of special mention for their contributions are Jack Ladd Carr of Maryland; Lynne Ianniello, the Anti-Defamation League of B'nai B'rith; Herbert M. Ames, president of the West Point Jewish Chapel; Dr. Malcolm H. Stern of the Park Avenue Synagogue; Dr. George Woodbridge of Rhode Island; Ken Kahn of Florida; Carla Rolde of Maine; F. Peter Rose and Albert Fried, both of New York City; and my friend and former colleague, the late Paul Greenfeder, the reference librarian of *The New York Times,* who was widely respected and loved for his ability and patience in the face of ever-pressing demands by impatient writers.

Dr. Jacob Rader Marcus, one of the country's finest American Jewish historians and the director of the American Jewish Archives in Cincinnati, Ohio, was kind enough to open his photographic files to the author. Without his kindness and the intelligent cooperation of Fannie Zelcer, his archivist, this book would have suffered greatly. Carl J. White, the secretary of J. & W. Seligman & Co., Inc., was a cordial and forthcoming source of information and of photographs for Part Five, as was George J. Fountaine of Guggenheim Brothers. The incomparable Gary M. Schuster of ASCAP supplied the unusual photographs that enliven the American Jewish songwriters of Part Six, and the New York Public Library was helpful throughout the project. Ruth MacGuffie assisted the author in picture research and proved invaluable.

Thomas Lask and Morris Harth, both of New York City, were the author's wise men, offering critical comments or soothing advice to a sometimes anxious writer. The opinions expressed in *Jewish America,* however, are the author's own and bear little resemblance to the counsel proffered by others.

The McGraw-Hill Book Company deserves special commendation for publishing an eccentric view of a sensitive subject, and my agile-minded editor, Ken Stuart, and his associates, PJ Haduch and Barbara Schindler Kastner, were more than equal to the task of guiding this complicated project through the many corridors of a large publishing house.

Seymour Kurtz

JEWISH AMERICA

PART ONE

◄ Isaac Aboab da Fonseca, the first rabbi in the New World. A Dutch Sephardic Jew, he arrived in Recife in 1642. (*American Jewish Archives, Cincinnati*)

From the Beginning

JEWS HAVE LIVED in America since its discovery by Columbus in 1492.

While this may seem an outrageous statement, it is nonetheless true. In fact, the first European to set foot on the first island reached by Columbus in the New World was Luis de Torres, his interpreter and a Spaniard of Jewish origin.

An intrepid linguist, Torres, who spoke Spanish, Hebrew, Aramaic, Arabic, and Latin, was sent forward by Columbus to parley with the brown-skinned and half-naked natives. After all, this was India, and its sufficiently civilized inhabitants would surely find at least one of Torres's many tongues intelligible. Of course, Columbus and his daring mariners were in the Bahamas, a long way from the riches and culture of India.

Though Torres's learning must have failed to impress the islanders of San Salvador, for so Columbus named it, the New World must have greatly impressed Torres, for he decided to settle there. Not on the small island of San Salvador, but on Cuba, the second island discovered by the Admiral of the Ocean Seas for Their Majesties Ferdinand and Isabella. Thus, according to recorded history, Luis de Torres was the first European settler in the New World.

At the outset this Jew of many languages traded with the friendly natives; later he established a tobacco plantation, becoming the first to introduce the use of the leaf into the Old World. Enchanted by the beauty and climate of Cuba, he invited his

Christopher Columbus, portrayed by an unknown seventeenth-
century artist. Columbus, whose true name was Cristóbal Colón,
was of Spanish Marrano descent. (*The New York Public Library*)

fellow Marranos—those Jews who were baptized as Christians but generally held to their ancient faith—to join him in that island paradise far from the bloody arms of the Spanish Inquisition. Torres never realized how long those arms really were.

There were several other Spanish Marranos with Columbus on his bold first voyage. Maestre Bernal, who had once undergone public humiliation in Valencia as a secret Jew, was Columbus's physician. The other former Jews included Marco, Columbus's chief surgeon, and Alonzo de la Calle from Jews' Street and Rodrigo Sánchez of Segovia, navigators and seafarers.

For Western historians the year 1492 marks the discovery of the New World, a momentous event in the world chronicle, but for Jews 1492 will long be remembered as a year of overwhelming disaster. In March of that year King Ferdinand of Aragón and his wife Queen Isabella of Castile decreed that any Jew found within the borders of Spain after July must accept baptism or suffer death, offering the ultimate choice between cross and sword. The 300,000 Jews of Spain, leaving the greater share of their worldly possessions behind, became a horde of refugees, seeking havens in other lands. Many perished or were sold as slaves; some were baptized by force. Children were torn from parents, and many Jewish mothers and fathers, to save their children from baptism, slew them and then themselves.

So struck by the event was Columbus himself that he began his personal journal as follows: "After the Spanish monarchs had expelled all the Jews from all their kingdoms and lands in January, in that same month they commissioned me to undertake the voyage to India with a properly equipped fleet."

Thousands of Jews were baptized during this period and stayed in Spain as conversos or Marranos. These were the New Christians, although more often than not they remained underground Jews, secretly loyal to the ancient beliefs of their fathers. Many noble Spanish families of today trace their lineage to Marrano ancestors.

From Phoenician times, centuries before the rise of Christianity, Jews had lived and

Their Most Catholic Majesties Ferdinand and Isabella. (*The New York Public Library*)

traded on the Iberian Peninsula. When the Moors conquered much of Spain in the eighth century, more and more Jews entered the country, where they prospered under a benign and tolerant Islam. As merchants and traders, scholars, physicians, poets, astronomers, and even advisers to caliphs and kings, Jews had made a singular contribution to Spanish life and culture.

In the ensuing centuries the Catholic Church grew more militant. Crusades were launched, and the reconquest of Spain was undertaken. By 1492, and the defeat of Islam in Granada, Spain was in Christian hands.

The dreaded edict of expulsion of 1492, issued by Their Most Catholic Majesties Ferdinand and Isabella, practically liquidated Judaism in Spain. It was the last of a series of harsh measures, backed by the royal house and the clergy, to rid Spain of Jews. For more than a century before, other methods had been employed: mob violence, public degradation, legal exclusion from certain trades and professions, and, finally, the seizure of Jewish property. This religious yearning for racial purity, strangely prophetic of what was to come in Nazi Germany, was blended with a strong mix of sharp-eyed greed. Many Spanish Jews were rich and influential, a situation that produced even more resentment against them than the religion they practiced openly or in secret.

As noted earlier, Jews in great numbers were compelled to accept baptism, creating a large population of New Christians. If, after renouncing Judaism, a Marrano reverted to the old way, he was considered a heretic and subjected to that appalling system of religious ministration, the infamous Spanish Inquisition.

The Inquisition, established in Spain in 1478 and unfortunately lasting until 1820, played a large part in early American Jewish history, not only because it relentlessly tracked Marranos even into the Spanish territories of the New World but because it served as a powerful motive for Spanish Jews to seek a new life in the Western Hemisphere.

The medieval inquisitions of Europe found their paragon in the Spanish Inquisition, as it

An auto-da-fé in seventeenth-century Spain. The burning of Marranos and other heretics was the church's most popular form of entertainment. (*The New York Public Library*)

Tomás de Torquemada, the Dominican monk who gave new meaning to the word *inquisition.* Torquemada, a fierce and inhuman zealot, was himself of Marrano origin. (*The New York Public Library*)

A page from the astronomical tables of Abraham Zacuto, published in Spain in 1473. Zacuto, a Spanish Jew, was a staunch supporter of Columbus at the Spanish royal court. Columbus used the Zacuto tables in his voyages of discovery. (*Jewish Theological Seminary of America, New York*)

| Tab eclipsis luminariuz et primo de sole | | | | | | | finis eclipsis | |
numer9 annornz	nomina mensiuz	dies	digiti	feria	hore	minut	hore	minu
1493	octob	10	9	5	0	0	1	20
1502	septeb	30	8	6	17	28	19	12
1506	Julii	20	3	2	1	49	3	3
1513	martii	7	4	1	23	49	1	9
1518	Junii	7	10	2	18	22	19	17
1524	Iannaz	23	9	2	3	12	4	6
Tabla de eclipsib9 lune								
1494	septeb	14	17	1	17	5	2	33
1497	Iannaz	18	17	4	3	50	7	18
1500	noueb	5	13	5	10	17	13	30
1501	maii	2	19	1	15	33	19	6
1502	octob	15	14	7	10	15	12	9
1504	februa	29	16	5	10	47	14	13
1505	aug9	14	15	5	5	42	9	6
1508	Junii	12	23	2	15	21	19	0
1509	Junii	2	7	7	9	29	2	3
1511	octob	6	13	2	9	11	2	25
1514	Iannaz	29	15	2	14	20	16	3
1515	Iannaz	19	15	7	5	0	6	42
1516	Julii	13	14	1	10	0	12	30
1519	noueb	6	20	1	5	50	6	48
1522	septeb	5	15	6	11	22	12	4
1523	martii	1	17	1	7	30	9	14

burgeoned under Ferdinand and Isabella. Its efficiency and brutality reached superior heights in the hands of Tomás de Torquemada, a Dominican monk whose rare gift for searching out clandestine Jews was surpassed only by his ferocious fanaticism.

As inquisitor general in 1492, the zealot monk was also confessor to the royal couple and the cloaked eminence behind the expulsion decree of that year. Torquemada himself was probably of Marrano origin, which would explain his savage crusade against secret Jews.

The distinguished American historian John Lothrop Motley offers a vivid description of the Inquisition at work:

> It arrested on suspicion, tortured till confession, and then punished by fire. . . . The torture took place at midnight, in a gloomy dungeon, dimly lighted by torches. The victim—whether man, matron or tender virgin—was stripped naked, and stretched upon the wooden bench. Water, weights, fire, pulleys, screws, all the apparatus by which the sinews could be strained without cracking, the bones crushed without breaking, and the body wracked exquisitely without giving up its ghost, was now put into operation. The executioner, enveloped in a black robe from head to foot, with his eyes glaring at his victim through holes cut in the hood which muffled his face, practiced successively all the forms of torture which the devilish ingenuity of the monks had invented.

The festive centerpiece of the Inquisition was the auto-da-fé, the so-called act of faith, when penitents from whom confessions had been tortured were publicly burned. It was a pageant, grotesquely awesome with its hooded masks and robes, its mass chanting and pious prayers. An auto-da-fé was a religious inspiration to all who attended: nobility and clergy, the fashionable and the poor. Thousands of Marranos were incinerated in this bizarre entertainment.

Once a center of culture and learning, Spain in 1492 was on the edge of financial disaster and in the sinister grip of the Inquisition.

Such was the kingdom of Ferdinand and Isabella when Columbus set forth on his great argosy.

Vexatious, and often acrimonious, is the scholarly debate surrounding the ancestral origin of Columbus himself. His affinity for Spanish Jews and Marranos, many of whom provided political and financial backing for his maritime project, is undeniable. Among these was Bishop Diego de Deza of Salamanca, theologian and Marrano, who championed Columbus's cause in the church and elsewhere. Abraham Senior, Isaac Abarbanel, Gabriel Sánchez, and Luis de Santángel, advisers to the Spanish throne and under its royal protection, gave substantial sums to Columbus. Santángel, chancellor of the royal household, granted Columbus his largest private contribution. A Jew by birth, Luis de Santángel was so esteemed by King Ferdinand that the monarch issued a decree exempting him, his wife, and their children and heirs from all and any charges brought by the Inquisition.

Among the Jews who offered the great navigator scientific aid were Abraham Zacuto, the learned astronomer, who publicly advocated Columbus's adventure and whose astronomical tables guided the course Columbus steered; Judah Cresques, an expert chart maker known as the Map Jew; and Levi ben Gershon, the inventor of nautical instruments.

Many historians, after years of scholarly research in the archives of Spain, Portugal, and Italy, have concluded that Cristóbal Colón, for such was Columbus's true name, was of Spanish Jewish descent. Salvador de Madariaga, the renowned Spanish historian, asserts in his authoritative biography of the inspired admiral that the family Colón, a common name among Jews in Spain, fled from persecution in Spain to Italy and settled in Genoa in about 1390, where some sixty years later Columbus was born. The Spanish Jewish, or Marrano, origin of Columbus, Madariaga further states, is supported by documentary evidence and provides the only viable explanation for the puzzling facts of Columbus's life, his sensitivity to the plight of Spanish Jewry and his intimate association with Spanish Jews and Marranos.

The Old Synagogue in Toledo, Spain. Toledo, once the seat of the Spanish monarchs, was a cultural center with a large Jewish quarter. After 1492, when the Jews were expelled from Spain, Toledo declined, and the synagogue was converted into a church. The synagogue-church was severely damaged during the Spanish Civil War, as can be seen in this unusual photograph. (*American Jewish Archives, Cincinnati*)

A rare engraving of Isaac Abarbanel, Spanish scholar and financier and one of Columbus's many Jewish and Marrano backers. (*Jewish Theological Seminary of America, New York*)

Other historians declare that the evidence is inconclusive.

Sadly, and apart from the fine points of scholarly discussion, Columbus died in penniless obscurity, forgotten and neglected by the Spanish crown. Generations later, when his accomplishments were better understood, his true greatness appeared.

Whatever the final judgment of history on Columbus as secret Jew, Marrano, or Italian Catholic, clearly Jews played a major role in the exploration and early settlement of the New World.

Jews, from the beginning, were uniquely suited to the American adventure. Their self-reliance, their resiliency, their bold spirit of enterprise, and their native astuteness were to serve America well in its long struggle for freedom, a goal both deeply felt and devoutly desired by Jews themselves. For who knew better than they the injustice and iniquity of the Old World?

Moritz Kayserling, the redoubtable German historian, asserts that where the history of the Jews in Spain ends, their history in America begins. The Inquisition, he further states, marks the last chapter of the professors of Judaism on the Iberian Peninsula and their opening chapter in the Western Hemisphere.

As knowledge of the newly discovered land spread, Jews and Marranos from Spain and Portugal were among the earliest settlers there. Relentless as was the Inquisition, many escaped its holy embrace. In 1502, just ten years after Columbus's first voyage of discovery, Queen Isabella issued her first royal license to trade in the New World ironically to Juan Sánchez, a Marrano whose father had been burned at the stake by the Inquisition.

These early settlers were, with few exceptions, Sephardic Jews whose roots were in the soil of Iberia, called *Sepharad* in Hebrew. The name distinguishes them from their coreligionists and future fellow settlers from Central and Eastern Europe, the Ashkenazim, who take their name from Germany, or *Ashkenaz* in Hebrew. Their story will unfold in the later pages of this chronicle.

Needless to say, the Spanish success did not go unnoticed by the European monarchs of the day, and a long struggle began for the possession and exploitation of the riches of the New World, with Spain, Portugal, France, Holland, and England in brutal contention. The Old World had forcibly projected itself into the Western Hemisphere with chilling effect.

By 1540 Spain was far in the lead: The opulent islands of Cuba, Jamaica, Puerto Rico, and Haiti were under the domination of Spanish conquistadors and soul-saving missionaries; Hernando Cortez had conquered Mexico and Francisco Pizarro, Peru; and Spain laid claim to Central America, Florida, the southwest region of North America, and almost all of South America. Brazil, however, with the coast towns of Recife (Pernambuco) and, a few years later, Bahia was held by Portugal.

During and after the Spanish Conquest millions of native Americans were exterminated by sword and fire and by overwork in the fields and mines. Cuba, Haiti, and Puerto Rico were virtually depopulated, and in Mexico and Peru, as well as in other Central and South American regions, whole towns were torched and every man, woman, and child slain. Genocide was never far from the mystical, rapacious Spanish soul.

Gold and silver, gems, tobacco and sugar, and slave labor were the royal plunder of the conquistadors, while Spanish missionaries, those fierce hunters after souls, sought salvation for their flocks, even if salvation meant the stake.

Many Jews and Marranos had ventured forth into the wide and distant spaces of Span-

Autos-da-fé were held regularly in Lima, Peru. In a sacred procession such as this Francisco Maldonado de Silva, the Jewish physician, was marched to his death in the seventeenth century. (*The New York Public Library*)

ish and Portuguese America, not only because the New World appealed to their spirit of enterprise but also because they could practice their ancient faith in freedom, beyond the reach and searching eye of the Inquisition—a pious longing never to be realized on the Spanish Main.

So many Sephardic Jews had reached the new Spanish territories by 1518 that the throne prohibited Marranos from departing from Spain for America, and a year later the church appointed a court of the Inquisition for the West Indies that would, at least in theory, protect the true Catholic faith in America from contamination by Jews, heretics, and infidels. These prohibitions and threats, offering the usual blend of piety and greed, proved ineffective, and in 1537 Pope Paul III issued a papal bull that forbade apostates, such as Jews, Marranos, and Protestants, from going to the Indies and that commanded his colonial bishops to expel them. At first feeble and tenuous, the Inquisition soon managed to uncoil its tentacles

An old print of Recife, Brazil, in the 1600s. "That city," the Portuguese church said, "is chiefly inhabited by Jews who have open synagogues there to the scandal of Christianity." One of those synagogues dominates the center of the print. (*American Jewish Archives, Cincinnati*)

and became a dominating power in Spanish and Portuguese colonies.

As early as 1528 the Spanish conquistador Hernando Alonso, one of Cortez's lieutenants, was executed in Mexico City for Jewish heresy. Several years later in New Mexico, a haven for Mexican Marranos, no less a person than the governor himself, Bernardo López de Mendizabal, came into conflict with the Inquisition, which charged him with having changed his linen on the eve of the Sabbath after he had washed his feet. A descendant of a known Jew, López de Mendizabal died in prison. His case is notable, being the first of its kind to occur in what is now the United States.

By 1570 the Inquisition was flourishing, especially in Mexico and Peru, those jewels of the Spanish crown. Secret agents were everywhere, prying into the lives of the New Christians for signs that they were not true believers. A smokeless chimney on the Jewish Sabbath, a festive family dinner at Passover time, a worn or hungry look on the Day of Atonement, or fresh clothes and a clean shirt on Saturday were enough to qualify a suspect for the Inquisition. It has been told that Jewish physicians frequently prescribed pork diets to their patients so as not to be suspected by the ferrets of the Holy Office.

In Peru, where Jews had risen to great affluence, much to the envy of their Catholic

Isaac Aboab da Fonseca, the first rabbi in the New World. A Dutch Sephardic Jew, he arrived in Recife in 1642. (*American Jewish Archives, Cincinnati*)

neighbors, many autos-da-fé were celebrated. One such burning featured Manuel Bautista Pérez, a Jew who was reputed to be the richest merchant in Lima. However, beyond all others, the story of the immolation of the surgeon Francisco Maldonado de Silva deserves to be retold.

Reared in Callao, the gateway port to Lima, Francisco was the son of Diego Núñez de Silva, a skilled surgeon and the descendant of an old Sephardic family. Diego as a youth had run afoul of the Inquisition and decided, with the better part of wisdom, to educate his children as Catholics. His son Francisco was also trained as a physician.

Francisco enjoyed a philosophical turn of mind and became greatly interested in theological discussion. The more he read and pondered the Bible and its commentaries, the more perplexed he became. He pressed his father for explanations, but the old man sought to avoid such discussions. Francisco was persistent, and finally Diego admitted the truth: that he himself was a Jew and had never really accepted the Christian faith. Thereafter, at Francisco's request, his father instructed him in Jewish traditions, beliefs, and practices. All this was a guarded secret, for the mere whisper of it would have exposed them to the gravest dangers.

In 1616 Diego Núñez de Silva died and was buried as a respected citizen and true son of the church. From then on Francisco pursued his Jewish studies alone.

A devoted son and husband, Maldonado de Silva, now a prominent physician and surgeon, lived happily with his wife and family and with his mother and sister. One day he decided to reveal the family secret to his sister, a devout Catholic. Shocked and sorely troubled, she sought the guidance of her priest, who insisted that she as a true daughter of the church must denounce her brother to the Inquisition. Reluctantly, but under her confessor's command, she tragically did so.

Francisco was immediately arrested and imprisoned. To his grim inquisitors he freely admitted his Judaism. Challenged, threatened, and cajoled by turns, the young physician defended his position with force and ingenuity

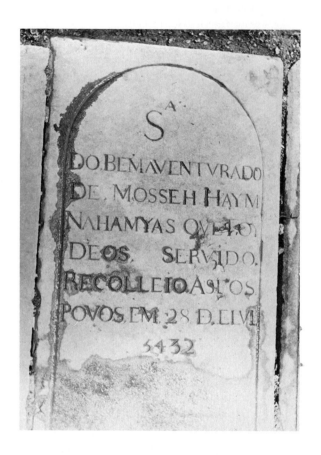

The gravestone of Moses Haym Nehemiah in Bridgetown, Barbados. Nehemiah was a Caribbean merchant who is said to have been the first pioneer trader in the colony of Virginia. While the inscription is in Latin, the death date is given in accordance with the ancient Jewish calendar; 5432 is 1672, our calendar. (*American Jewish Archives, Cincinnati*)

and remained adamant. For nearly thirteen terrible years in prison he refused to swear on the cross, rejected conversion, stood his ground against the priests of the Holy Office, and bore his sufferings heroically. He was a Jew, he repeated to his priestly wardens, and would live and die as such. His refusal to bend in the face of inexorable inquisitorial power was a constant inspiration to his fellow prisoners, of whom there were many.

Finally in sheer monkish frustration, Francisco Maldonado de Silva was committed to an auto-da-fé. In 1639 de Silva, by then little more than a walking skeleton, was burned at the stake in what was reported to be one of Lima's great galas. Thus was executed the most famous of American Jewish martyrs and an apostle of religious liberty in the New World.

IN THE DECADES prior to and after the expulsion order of 1492 thousands of Sephardic Jews had furtively settled in Holland and had willingly supported Protestant causes. With the Utrecht Union of 1579, which freed the Protestant Netherlands from Catholic Spain, clandestine Jews could show their true colors. There they emerged as a strong Jewish community, which supported the Dutch against their inveterate enemy, the Spanish. This alliance between the Jews and Dutch was to provide the foundations of religious tolerance in the Low Countries. Though not full citizens, the Jews of Holland, who had made significant contributions to the building of this small but powerful country, were accorded many fundamental civil and economic liberties. By the 1650s Amsterdam was the commercial center of Europe, the Dutch

The Old Jewish Cemetery in St. Thomas, the Virgin Islands. It dates from the 1600s. (*American Jewish Archives, Cincinnati*)

colonial empire extended into the New World, and Jews had found a reasonably safe haven. Dutch Jews, sheltered by the state, were to form the most cultured and prosperous Jewish community of its time. In it was Baruch Spinoza, the philosopher, whose advanced ideas caused his expulsion from that same community; the Jews of Holland had not forgotten their Iberian heritage.

IN NONE of Spain's New World territories was there an open, practicing Jewish community. Conditions were somewhat better in Portuguese Brazil, where New Christians, or Marranos, were trading as early as 1510. Lax and vacillating in its policy toward these suspected heretics, the Portuguese crown, unlike the Spanish, more or less suffered the growing influx of Sephardic Jews into its chief colony, perhaps foolishly. For within a century these enterprising underground Jews were prominent planters, merchants, brokers, and professional men and Recife and Bahia, Brazil's major coastal cities, were covertly but heavily Jewish. Sugar growing, the mainstay of the Brazilian economy, had been introduced in 1548 by Jewish planters from Madeira.

In 1621 the Dutch West India Company, organized for trade, colonization, and conquest in the Western Hemisphere, was founded, and there ensued a series of wars with Portugal for control of the rich and vast expanses of Brazil, a continuing struggle in which the Marranos of Brazil and the Jews of Holland had a vital stake. If the Dutch won, the Jews of Brazil would be free from the menacing shadow of the church and its Inquisition and free finally to be themselves.

In 1624 the Dutch, stretching their maritime power, reached out and seized Bahia from the Portuguese. Several hundred Marranos openly welcomed them, affirmed their Judaism, and proclaimed their allegiance to Holland. This was a day of darkness, for the Portuguese reconquered the city within the year and gave the premature rejoicers severe cause for regret. Six years later the tireless Dutch struck again, this time at Recife, which proved a much

Mikveh Israel in Curaçao, the oldest existing synagogue in the Western Hemisphere. It was built in 1732. (*American Jewish Archives, Cincinnati*)

greater prize than Bahia. Thousands of Marranos, long suppressed by their Portuguese overlords, threw off their guise of Catholicism and promptly established an open and vigorous Jewish community, the first in the New World. Jews from Spanish America, from other parts of Brazil, and from Holland flocked to Recife to breathe its fresh, free air, and the city, now greatly enlarged, prospered.

By 1642 Recife Jewry was well established, and a professional rabbi, who was to be its

while Jews and Dutch alike fought valiantly against the common enemy but to little avail. In January 1654, after an unendurable siege, during which Rabbi Isaac Aboab went about encouraging the weary soldiers and their hungry families, Recife was starved into surrender. Its proud and singular Jewish community came to a sharp end. The Brazilian Jews were expelled from the very land they had helped build, from their homes, from their fields and sugar plantations, from their mills and factories and from their synagogues, which were destroyed.

A miniature exodus followed the Portuguese victory; while a few Jews returned to underground life, others fled to Holland. Most sought to resettle in the Dutch, English, and French colonies of the Caribbean. Surinam (or Dutch Guiana), Cayenne, and the Dutch island of Curaçao were most favored by the Brazilian exiles. The English colony of Jamaica, wrested from the Spanish in 1655, already had a number of Spanish and Portuguese Marranos, who were soon joined by their Brazilian cousins. The British permitted the Jews to remain but taxed them heavily and restricted their civil liberties. The merchants of London hoped to limit Jewish competition. On the British island of Barbados Jewish refugees were received, but they were not granted official toleration.

Asylum was also sought in Guadaloupe, Martinique, and Saint Christopher in the West Indies, where for decades a struggle had waxed between the Jesuits and the French colonial authority over the future of French Jews already settled in the islands. Almost all the prosperous maritime trade was in Jewish hands, but the Jesuits were driving for expulsion since, from their half-sighted view, all Jews were the avowed enemies of Catholicism. The colonial authorities, not to be swayed by religious argument when revenues were involved, circumvented Jesuit opposition, and some 900 Jews were permitted to enter, although unofficially and with caution.

Within a few years the Jewish connection in the West Indies, by then firmly established, was destined to provide a bountiful commercial harvest for their less sophisticated brethren in colonial North America, in such small ports as

spiritual teacher and leader, was summoned from Amsterdam. A talmudic scholar, author and orator, Isaac Aboab da Fonseca was the first rabbi in the Americas. The learned Isaac Aboab issued a translation of the Bible in Portuguese in 1649 for the many Portuguese Marranos who could not read Hebrew.

Two synagogues were built in Recife, and for its flourishing Jewish community freedom and prosperity seemed assured. However, this rosy dream was to turn into a nightmare. The Portuguese, who had too long suffered Dutch colonial expansion at their expense, decided to retake Recife since that city, according to the church, was an abomination where Jews publicly worshiped their God to the scandal of Christianity. For nine years the war continued,

New York, Newport, Philadelphia, Charleston, and Savannah.

From the many rich ports on the Spanish Main and in the Caribbean galleons and caravels laden with treasure and with sugar, cotton, cocoa, and tobacco plied the seas. Beyond the greediest dreams of the European host, which had descended on the New World in search of plunder, was the wealth of the Americas. For the Jew the bright promise of a new world was tarnished by the noxious fumes of violence and prejudice from the old; he was still shunned and persecuted as an outcast. Gifted entrepreneurs and successful adventurers, eminently suited for frontier colonial life, the American Jews still longed for nothing less than religious, civil, and social justice, hallmarks of the Jewish spirit from time immemorial.

The year 1654 stands as a key date in American Jewish history, not only because of the Portuguese reconquest of Brazil and the subsequent upheaval in the European colonies of the West Indies, but surely because in September of that year twenty-three "penniless but healthy" Dutch and Portuguese Jews, travel-weary refugees from the Caribbean, arrived uninvited at the Dutch colonial port of New Amsterdam. A rude village sited on the lower tip of Manhattan, New Amsterdam was to become, despite itself, the locus of the first permanent Jewish settlement in the United States.

PART TWO

◀ New Amsterdam, the Dutch colony precariously perched on the tip of Manhattan Island, in 1656. Jews had settled in the colony two years before this view was rendered. The *St. Charles,* which transported the new arrivals from the West Indies, is often called the Jewish *Mayflower.* (*American Jewish Archives, Cincinnati*)

The Thirteen Colonies

IN THE GREAT American Southwest Spanish Marranos partici-
pated in the sixteenth-century conquest of the territory, long
before John Smith dreamed of Jamestown, Virginia, and before
the Pilgrims set foot on Plymouth Rock. On the eastern seaboard,
where the thirteen colonies were to flourish, Jewish traders, probably from the West Indies, wandered the wilderness, bartering
goods with the Indians. Some of the first trade outposts in North
America may have been Jewish in origin.

Since historic evidence for that period is scant, especially
where the earliest Jewish American pioneers are concerned, it is
best to follow the witty admonition of Jacob Rader Marcus, the
fine American scholar, who warns: "The careful historian soon
comes to the unfailing rule that no Jew is ever the first Jew in
any place: there is always one who had been there before him."

When the twenty-three Jewish pilgrims from the Caribbean
disembarked from the French schooner *St. Charles,* they were
greeted with less than enthusiasm by the 1,500 hard-bitten souls
of New Amsterdam. The town, which was to become New York
in ten years, was unprepossessing in appearance with neither the
wealth or ambience of old Amsterdam nor the warmth, color,
and prosperity of the older Caribbean ports.

New Amsterdam was an isolated Dutch community,
blocked on the land side by neighboring English colonies but
open to the sea for trade and sustenance. It was the frequent
target of Algonquin Indian raids.

Founded in 1625 by the Dutch West India Company, some thirty years before the arrival of our refugee Jews, it was designated the capital of New Netherland, a vague colonial region that was fortified against English incursions by Dutch hope rather than by power.

Peter Minuit, the first director general of New Netherland, purchased Manhattan from the Indians for trinkets valued at $24 and named it New Amsterdam. This was the first of many real estate coups that were to make Manhattan Island famous in the annals of American history.

New Amsterdam by 1654 had earned a reputation as a fur trade center, chiefly for its beaver pelts, then the fashion rage of Europe, and for its natural harbor on the Hudson River. Furs in exchange for beads, textiles, and metal tools lay at the heart of the hazardous Indian trade. A provincial and xenophobic town on the edge of the wilderness, New Amsterdam was cluttered with little Dutch houses and in-

Peter Stuyvesant of New Amsterdam, the most irascible bigot of his time. (*American Jewish Archives, Cincinnati*)

tersected by paths and lanes that dissolved into ooze when it rained. It boasted a windmill; a church—Dutch Reformed, of course; a fort, on the site of the Battery; a warehouse and pier; and a tavern, which also served as the town hall. On the northern limit of the town stood the fortified wooden palisade called the *waal;* along its base ran a path which has since become known to the world as Wall Street.

Such was the cheerless view that greeted the small band of weary Jews as they left the vessel *St. Charles;* the master of the ship hastened to auction their belongings to pay for the cost of their passage.

Peter Stuyvesant, who had lost a leg in the colonial wars of Curaçao, was then director

Chatham Square Cemetery in lower Manhattan was established in the 1680s and is probably the oldest existing Jewish burial ground in the United States. (*American Jewish Archives, Cincinnati*)

An interesting view of colonial Manhattan from its southern tip to the forests and woodlands above Canal Street. Much of the harbor's shipping was handled by Jewish merchants. (*The New York Public Library*)

general of New Netherland and ran the colony as his autocratic fief. An irascible bigot, he despised all Protestant sects other than Dutch Reformed but positively loathed Catholics, Quakers, and Jews, in that order. One can only imagine the expression on Stuyvesant's face when he was informed that twenty-three penurious Jews had arrived in his town.

Giving vent to his spleen, the testy director general at first attempted persuasion, but when the Jews refused to believe that there was no room for them on Manhattan Island, he personally undertook to have them expelled. Supported by his coreligionists, he petitioned the directors of the Dutch West India Company for an official order of expulsion on the ground that "the deceitful race—such hateful enemies and blasphemers of the name of Christ—be not allowed further to infect and trouble this new colony."

New York, in North America.

Alarmed at the prospect of expulsion, the new immigrants, who had as Jews been accorded official toleration by the Dutch government years before, immediately appealed to their Jewish brethren in old Amsterdam, many of whom were large stockholders and even directors of the company.

After much delay, caused in large part by the slowness of ships' mail, the company finally responded to the impatient Stuyvesant: Jews, his masters ordered, "may travel and trade to and in New Netherland and live and remain there, provided the poor among them shall not become a burden to the Company or to the community, but be supported by their own nation."

Stuyvesant, still unconvinced and bitter, argued: "Giving them liberty, we cannot refuse the Lutherans and Papists." The directors of the company curtly closed the discussion by stating that their directive did not include the free exercise of religion: "The consent given to the Jews to go to New Netherland and there to enjoy the same liberty that is granted to them in this country was extended with respect to civil and political liberties. . . ."

Overjoyed and relieved by the company's decision, the small Jewish community of Manhattan was legally free to go about its business, but the egregious prohibition against religious liberty was to grow more and more repugnant in Jewish eyes. However, it should be remembered that the charter of Jewish settlement granted by the Dutch was the first of its kind in the United States.

Peter Stuyvesant and his cohorts, still nursing bruises from the Jewish skirmish, were not willing to forgive and forget in true Christian fashion. The company was an ocean away after all, and its directives were not always explicit about Jewish rights, so Stuyvesant and his council of elders were able to indulge their spite. Unusual taxes were levied on the Jews of New Amsterdam; ownership of land, as well as freedom to trade, was restricted; and the holding of public office and service in the militia were denied.

Among the handful of refugees aboard the *St. Charles* was one Asser Levy van Swellem, a native of Amsterdam who had settled in Recife but fled after the Portuguese reconquest. An ardent Dutch Jew, bristling with democratic fervor, Levy challenged and fought the embittered Stuyvesant and his council at every turn. He demanded nothing less than burgher rights, or the full rights of a Dutch citizen. In this undertaking he was supported by Jacob Barsimson, usually regarded as New Amsterdam's first Jewish settler.

Barsimson, who had arrived from Holland aboard *De Pereboom* (*The Peartree*), three weeks before the *St. Charles* discharged its unwanted refugees, had received a Jewish allotment from Peter Stuyvesant, an old hut outside the wall. At first a manual laborer, he gradually worked himself into the Indian trade.

Together Asser Levy and Jacob Barsimson provided the hapless Jewish community with an assertive voice that must have given Stuyvesant and his council a giant migraine. In 1655, just a year after their arrival, Levy and Barsimson petitioned for the right to stand watch in defense of the town, like other burghers. This was promptly denied with the sarcastic rejoinder that if they thought the council's refusal was injurious, they were herewith granted permission "to depart whenever and whither it please them." Not to be denied, Levy and Barsimson, both young and able-bodied men, volunteered their services to the head of the colonial militia, who, short of manpower, happily accepted, bringing the Jews of New Amsterdam that much closer to full burgher status. The resolute Levy and Barsimson were soon joined in the struggle for equal rights by such large Jewish taxpayers and men of substance as Abraham DeLucena, Jacob Cohen Henricque, Salvador Dandrada, Joseph d'Acosta, and David Frera. Despite Stuyve-

Jacob Philadelphia, named for the city by his proud parents, is said to have been the first Jewish boy born in the City of Brotherly Love. In later life he became a prominent inventor in Germany. (*American Jewish Archives, Cincinnati*)

William Penn, the great founder of Philadelphia, in 1682. A believing and practicing Quaker, he opened the doors of his settlement to Jews. (*American Jewish Archives, Cincinnati*)

James Oglethorpe, the founder of Savannah. He admitted Jews to the colony in 1733, despite the objections of his colonial trustees. (*The New York Public Library*)

sant's surly prohibitions against Jewish enterprise and his unfair tax practices, some Jews prospered; seven Jews, five of whom are named, representing one-thirtieth of the total defense tax roll, paid a disproportionate one-twelfth of the whole.

This band of activists petitioned one and all. And in 1656 the Dutch West India Company took final action: The stubborn Stuyvesant was reprimanded and categorically ordered to permit Jews to buy and own real estate and to trade freely as far north as the tiny Dutch settlement of Fort Orange (now Albany, New York) and along the Hudson and Delaware rivers.

Still dragging his feet, Stuyvesant waited for almost a year before he authorized the burgomasters of New Amsterdam to admit the Jews of the town to burghership. The building of a synagogue was not permitted.

The Jews of New Amsterdam, who successfully fought for civil and political equality in that frontier town, not only obtained benefits for themselves but also cleared the way for the aspirations of other disenfranchised peoples, soon to arrive in Manhattan.

Asser Levy had become by the time of his death in 1681 one of the wealthiest men in New York and probably the most prominent Jew in the colonies. He dared trade in furs in the days when the fur trade was a Dutch Christian monopoly and had earned such respect from the New Amsterdam authorities for his advocacy of Jewish causes that he was selected as one of six licensed butchers for the town but was expressly excused from killing hogs. So much had times changed.

In 1662 Levy acquired land on William Street and thus became one of the first Jewish landowners in what is now the United States. He also bought land in Albany. Levy prospered and won a recognized position for himself in the Dutch community.

When the English took New Amsterdam in 1664, renaming it New York, Levy, his reputation well established, continued his successful career. A good and honorable citizen, he took upon himself many neighborly duties for Christian and Jew alike. In 1671, when the Lu-

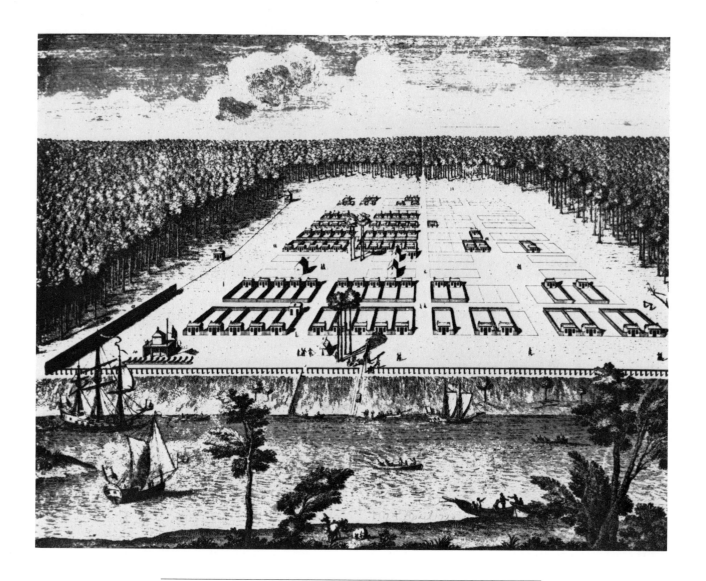

An eighteenth-century print of the building of Savannah. Jews were already settled there, and John Wesley, the father of Methodism, said of them that they "seem nearer the mind that was in Christ than many of those who call Him Lord." (*The New York Public Library*)

therans built their first church in New York, Levy advanced them the funds. On several occasions he acted as executor for his many Christian friends, and even the municipal court called upon him to act as trusted custodian of goods awaiting litigation. Levy built a public slaughterhouse on Wall Street in 1678. Historians sometimes regard this as the symbolic precursor of the New York Stock Exchange.

His grandson Asser Levy fought for the patriotic cause as an ensign of the First New Jersey Regiment in the Revolutionary War. Young Levy followed in the footsteps of his grandfather, another fighter for liberty who must rank among the first of the truly genuine Americans.

Director General Stuyvesant, after the surrender of New Amsterdam, grumpily retired to his farm, the Bouwerie, in lower Manhattan. It covered much of what is now the Lower East Side, which, in an ironic twist of fate, was to become in the early 1900s a famous center of Yiddish speakers and Yiddish culture. The Dutchman was buried on his farm in 1672, beneath his private chapel, now the site of St. Mark's in the Bowery, at Second Avenue and Tenth Street.

When in 1664 four English men-of-war, laden with troops and heavy guns, forced the capitulation of New Amsterdam, the Dutch military presence in North America was ended. New Netherland was divided into two colonies, known as New York and New Jersey, a division that brought the number of English colonies in the United States to thirteen prior to 1776. From New Hampshire to Georgia, the English were to hold sway.

Their new masters permitted the Jews of New York to retain the rights they had laboriously won from the Dutch. They were forbidden, however, to engage in retail trade or to practice a craft, for here they would be in direct competition with their Christian neighbors; to worship their God publicly; or to hold public office. As onerous as these restrictions seem now, they were, in fact, not very formidable. The English rarely enforced the prohibitions, and the Jews were content to worship in the privacy of their homes. They entered the retail trade as peddlers and were too busy making livings to aspire to public office. Furthermore, if they possessed crafts, they practiced them since craftsmen were in great demand. All in all, the rights granted to the Jews of New York by the Dutch, often under duress, and affirmed by the English surpassed those enjoyed by Jews in the other English colonies.

In the Massachusetts Bay colony, for example, Jews were not even permitted to settle in the early days. Solomon Franco, a Jewish wanderer in Massachusetts, was ordered back to Holland in 1649. In that same year Maryland, founded by Catholics, passed a for-Christians-only Toleration Act. Those who denied the divinity of Christ were guilty of blasphemy, for which the penalty was death. The "Jew doctor" Jacob Lumbrozo, who had foolishly settled in Maryland, was accused of that crime, impris-

oned, but was saved from death by a general amnesty.

A curious example of colonial Puritan mentality was shown in Connecticut in 1670. Jacob Lucena, a Jewish fur trader from New York, tried to deal in Connecticut but ran afoul of the law. Whether he was ahead of his time or had simply spent too many lonely hours in the wilderness, Lucena was charged with having been "notorious in his lascivious dalience

A nineteenth-century version of Dr. Samuel Nunez ministering to the sick of Savannah. It is reported that Nunez, a Sephardic physician, halted a fierce epidemic in Savannah in the 1740s. (*American Jewish Archives, Cincinnati*)

and wanton carriage and profers to severall women." Found guilty of lust, he was fined £20 by the court, a substantial sum. Lucena appealed to the Puritan magistrates, strict believers in the Hebrew Scriptures, who responded to his plea by reducing his fine by half because he was a Jew and therefore one of God's Chosen.

Jewish trading posts along the Delaware River stretched into southeastern Pennsylvania and had been established some years before the arrival of William Penn in 1682. Philadelphia, founded as a liberal Quaker city, was to become a center of Jewish life in America in the eighteenth century.

South Carolina's constitution was framed by the great John Locke and guaranteed freedom of conscience to all, including "Jews, heathens and disenters." And Jews sailed into the port of Charleston as early as the 1680s. Simon Valentine, a Jewish merchant, became police constable of Charleston in 1699, and in the general election of 1702 Carolina Jews voted for the first time.

James Oglethorpe, who in 1733 established the colony of Georgia, ignored the prejudice of his colonial trustees and admitted Jews to Savannah, a few months after the town was founded. Benjamin Sheftall, a German Jew who became a Georgia planter, kept a diary of that period in Hebrew, and Samuel Nunez, a Jewish physician, put a stop to an epidemic in Savannah "so that not one died afterwards." John Wesley, the father of Methodism, visited the

Isaac De Lyon, a member of the famous De Lyon family of Charleston. Jews were settled in Charleston in the 1690s. (*American Jewish Archives, Cincinnati*)

The tombstone of "the Right Reverend" Moses Cohen, a rabbi in Charleston in the mid-eighteenth century; his death date is given as 1762. (*American Jewish Archives, Cincinnati*)

Moses Levy, merchant prince and wealthy shipowner in colonial
New York. Levy, a rich colonial, emulated the dress of the English
nobility. (*American Jewish Archives, Cincinnati*)

Jews of Savannah in 1737 and wrote in his journal that they "seem nearer the mind that was in Christ than many of those who call Him Lord."

Although a few Jews had settled in Virginia as early as 1621, a year after the Pilgrim Fathers landed in Massachusetts, they played an inconspicuous role in the Virginia colony, dominated by great landowners who lived the life of English gentlemen cultivating their estates by slave labor. However, among the Jews of early Virginia was a successful physician, John de Sequeyra, who believed that the consumption of large amounts of tomatoes would lead to immortality. He was surely the first of America's many diet doctors. It was not until 1790 that Virginia's first Jewish congregation was established in Richmond.

In the vast French territory of Louisiana, far from the centers of British North America, Jews had settled prior to 1724, but little is known of them. The *Code Noir* of that year, issued by the French royal governor, ordered that the directors of the Louisiana Company "chase out of said country all Jews who have established their residence there. . . ." Whether or not the proclamation was effective is unknown.

Before we turn to the outstanding Jewish community of Newport, Rhode Island, destined to become a glittering light in colonial America, the Jews of New York deserve further attention. Some, such as the Gomez, Robles, Levy, De-Lucena, Franks, Michaels, and Pacheco families, prospered under their new English overlords, while others suffered civil and legal disabilities. Rabba Couty, a New York Jewish burgher, for example, had his ketch impounded and its cargo confiscated by the English in Jamaican waters in 1671 because he was a Jew and thus an alien.

Saul Brown, in 1685, was prohibited from opening a retail shop in New York because in his case the authorities felt it proper to hold him to the strict letter of the law. He had been acting as rabbi to the small Jewish congregation. Brown, whose real name was Pardo, meaning "brown" in Spanish, was among the first Jewish Americans to Anglicize their names, a vogue that continues into the present.

Another Jew of little means was Joseph Isacks, who, as it turns out, was probably the first Jew to bear arms for the British in North America. He enlisted in the militia during King William's War, which lasted from 1689 to 1697. In that war, the first of many between the English and the French for domination of the American continent and its lucrative trade, the luckless Isacks lost his musket; the report of the loss still exists.

The wealthy Jews of New York were engaged in the fur trade, in risky sea ventures, trafficking with the West Indies, Europe, and the Madeiras, and in real estate investments. Bold enterprisers, these merchant shippers and traders were to supply the venture capital and the energy that would bring the port of New York to world prominence.

Benjamin Gomez, one of the younger sons of the highly respected Luis Moses Gomez, merchant shipper, fur trader, and pioneer in colonial New York. (*American Jewish Historical Society, Waltham, Mass.*)

An interior view of the
Gomez House. (*Demetry*)

The Gomez House, the oldest existing Jewish residence in the
United States, as it looks today. It was built in 1714 by Luis
Moses Gomez as an Indian trading post near Newburgh, New
York. (*Demetry*)

In 1700 Richard Coote, Earl of Bellomont, the governor of New York, New Hampshire, and Massachusetts, wrote to his government in England "that, were it not for one Dutch merchant and two or three Jews that have let me have money, I should have been undone." Eleven years later seven New York Jews contributed to the building of a steeple atop Trinity Church on lower Broadway in Manhattan. The oldest and most beautiful of Anglican churches in America, it was founded in 1697. The Jewish gift bears testimony to the budding American spirit of tolerance and mutual respect that contrasted sharply with the old hatreds of Europe. It should be borne in mind that about the time the steeple was being built, in Portugal and in Poland Jewish men and women were being burned at the stake or quartered alive.

Among the special contributors to Trinity Church were Moses Levy, Luis Moses Gomez, and Jacob Franks, three of the most powerful Jewish patriarchs in the colonies. Moses Levy, no relation to the Asser Levy of Dutch times, was an English Jew who settled in New York about 1695. He arrived with money, overseas connections, and a growing family. He was to marry twice and father twelve children, many of whom became distinguished Americans, as did their children after them.

Levy was a merchant prince and ship-owner, real estate investor, and distiller. His progeny included Hayman Levy, a leading fur trader and at one time the employer of the German immigrant John Jacob Astor; Samson Levy, a prominent Philadelphia merchant; Nathan Levy, founder of the Philadelphia Jewish congregation; and several other Levy descendants active in the early settlements of Newport and Baltimore. Moses Levy, the grandson of the old patriarch, was considered by Thomas Jefferson for the cabinet post of attorney general.

A word more about Hayman, or Haym, Levy. He became the largest fur trader in the colonies, with trappers and hunters opening up wilderness lands that would someday become the states of Ohio, West Virginia, Kentucky, Indiana, and Illinois. Indians brought their finest furs to Levy's headquarters in New York City, and at certain seasons they and their furs were to be seen lining the streets to his warehouse. He was not only the first employer of young John Jacob Astor, generator of the Astor millions, who received $1 a day for cleaning pelts, but also of Nicholas Low. Ancestor of Seth Low, who was to become president of Columbia University, Nicholas Low served as Levy's clerk for seven years. Low began his own great fortune with Levy's financial assistance.

Luis Moses Gomez was the son of Isaac Gomez, a Spanish Marrano nobleman who about 1660 was forced to flee Spain for France because of the Inquisition. Luis Moses later left France to escape growing persecution, and some years before 1703 he and his six sons were settled in New York. Well connected, Luis Gomez, then the head of a large family business, was granted a royal document by Queen Anne that permitted him to conduct trade anywhere in the British colonies. The family was widely known for its daring enterprise in merchant shipping and in Indian trading.

The physical hazards to which seafaring merchants of that day were exposed are illustrated by the tragic fate of Jacob Gomez, one of Luis Gomez's sons. He had taken a load of goods to Cuba, and while the cargo was being offloaded, a band of Spaniards surprised the crew, killed the captain, and hacked Jacob Gomez to death.

In 1714 Luis Gomez purchased about 2,500 acres of land on the Hudson, just north of Newburgh, New York. There he, in pursuit of the Indian trade, built a fieldstone trading post at the point where several Indian trails converged; it was near a stream that became known as Jew's Creek. Furs obtained from the Indians were carried down to a landing on the Hudson and then shipped downriver to the port of New York. The fortlike house, with stone walls almost three feet thick, still stands, though enlarged by later owners. The Gomez House is the oldest colonial Jewish residence still to be seen in this country and is listed in the National Register of Historic Places.

Jacob Franks, young, bright, and ambitious, was sent to New York in 1710 by his rich kinfolk in London. Two years later he mar-

Jacob Franks, an outstanding entrepreneur in the colonial trade, was wise enough to marry the daughter of Moses Levy, thus uniting two moneyed Jewish families. (*American Jewish Archives, Cincinnati*)

David and Phila Franks, the young children of Jacob Franks.
David, a Tory, was to be harassed during the American
Revolution, and Phila shocked colonial Jewry when she married
Oliver De Lancey, the scion of a wealthy gentile family. (*American
Jewish Archives, Cincinnati*)

ried Abigail Levy, the daughter of the merchant prince Moses Levy. A large family grew, as did Franks's fortune. By the 1730s he was one of the most prominent merchant shippers of the city, the king's agent for New York and the northern colonies, and a major purveyor of supplies to the British army during the French and Indian Wars, which lasted for more than seventy years. At his death in 1769 Jacob Franks was accounted to be among the richest men, if not the richest man, in the colonies.

David Franks, one of Jacob's sons, became a leading merchant and politician in Philadelphia. In his early years he was very active in land speculation in Pennsylvania, Virginia, and some western lands, but he gained celebrity as the supplier of army goods to Colonel George Washington and his Virginia militia, who in 1758 were attacking Fort Duquesne in western Pennsylvania. In a letter from the young officer to Franks, the honest Washington inquires of the Philadelphia merchant: "I must beg to know how our paper money passes with you; for I suppose I shall be under the necessity of paying in that currency, having little of another kind with us. I hope you will excuse the liberty I have here taken, without *first* knowing whether it would be agreeable to you." Franks accepted the paper scrip.

A loyal subject of the British crown at the time of the Revolution, he was twice tried for being a Tory, imprisoned, and then expelled from Philadelphia. As a Jew he maintained only tenuous contact with colonial Jewry, a situation that sorely grieved his father, Jacob, an Orthodox Jew. In 1793 David died in a yellow fever epidemic.

Intermarriage among the great Jewish families of the time was commonplace, and a network of relatives and friends of relatives arose not only in the major ports of the colonies—Newport, New York, Philadelphia, Charleston, and Savannah—but in such faraway places as Lisbon, London, Amsterdam, Hamburg, and the West Indies. These interfamily ties promoted commerce and trade, concentrated capital, and,

Woodford, the home of David Franks in Philadelphia, where the son of Jacob Franks became rich as a supplier of arms and goods to the British army. (*American Jewish Archives, Cincinnati*)

above all, preserved an island of Judaism in a rising sea of Christianity. In New York, as elsewhere, Jewish merchants played second best to the gentile establishment. Families such as the De Lanceys, Clintons, Pelhams, Van Cortlandts, Beekmans, Warrens, and Morrises, as intermarried as their Jewish financial peers, were the real arbiters of social and political power in New York.

It should be noted that most Jews, like other colonial Americans, were in the poor to modest economic class. They were failed merchants, struggling farmers, manual laborers, tailors, shoemakers, soldiers and sailors, craftsmen, bakers and butchers. Unfortunately the pages of history tend to ignore these humble but dependable people for the glamour of the wealthy and the mighty. Nothing succeeds like success in American life.

Under English rule restrictions against public worship were gradually relaxed. In any case Jews had been meeting covertly in a house on Beaver Street to practice their ancient religion. Prior to 1700 the Jews of New York had formed Shearith Israel, the Remnant of Israel, which remains the oldest Jewish congregation in the United States.

After much bickering with the authorities, Congregation Shearith Israel was granted leave to build a public house of worship. Luis Gomez, Jacob Franks, the Levys, and other pillars of Jewish society provided the funds, and in 1730 the first synagogue in North America was dedicated on Mill Street. In ever-developing Manhattan neither street nor synagogue survived; however, the congregation presently prospers as the Spanish and Portuguese Synagogue, off Central Park West in Manhattan.

An old print of the Mill Street Synagogue, first to be erected in this country. Built in 1730 in downtown Manhattan, it housed Congregation Shearith Israel. (*The New York Public Library*)

The Spanish and Portuguese Synagogue on Central Park West in Manhattan, the current home of Shearith Israel, the oldest Jewish congregation in the United States. (*American Jewish Archives, Cincinnati*)

ROGER WILLIAMS, the radical advocate of religious freedom, was banished from the Massachusetts Bay colony in 1635. Within a few years he had founded the colony of Rhode Island and Providence Plantations on Narragansett Bay, which was to become a refuge for religious dissenters. Of great personal charm and unquestioned integrity, Williams was a friend to any who differed with the religious establishments.

Speaking of his liberal policy toward Jews, Williams said, "I desire not that liberty to myself which I would not freely and impartially weigh out to all the consciences of the world besides." Bitter resentment against Williams and his Jews of Newport was expressed by Cotton Mather, that learned bigot and heresy hunter from Massachusetts, who pointed to Newport as "the common receptacle of the convicts of Jerusalem and the outcasts of the land."

Roger Williams, founder of the colony of Rhode Island, welcomed religious dissenters and Jews to his domain. (*The New York Public Library*)

Attracted by the hope of religious liberty, fifteen Jewish families from Holland arrived in Newport in 1658, just four years after the *St. Charles* had docked in New Amsterdam. There is little evidence of Jewish communal life until 1677, when cemetery land was purchased. This has become the oldest recorded Jewish burial ground in the United States; Newport, after New York, was the earliest organized Jewish community in this country. The Jews of Newport were to play a leading role in the growing prosperity of the town, which, for a time, even surpassed the eminence of New York as a port and commercial center.

In 1685, two years after Roger Williams died, a Major William Dyre, supported by envious gentile merchants, brought charges against the Jews as aliens, and the property of Jewish merchants was seized. This was a bald attempt to drive the Jews out of business; there were snakes even in the Garden of Eden. On March 31, 1685, the Newport magistrates, in their greater wisdom, resorted to a legal technicality to decide in favor of one of the town's chief economic assets, the Jews.

By the 1750s Spanish and Portuguese Jews from Iberia and the West Indies, those daring Marrano adventurers, had arrived in Newport, and soon the city sheltered a thriving Jewish community. A booming prosperity followed in shipbuilding, in whaling and the whale oil industry, in rum and molasses, and in the abominable slave traffic. The wealth, social prominence, and generosity of Newport's Jews were heralded throughout the world of Jewry and soon drew emissaries from impoverished Jewish communities elsewhere. It is a centuries-old tradition that wealthy Jews help those who are otherwise.

In 1759 the Newport congregation of Jeshuat Israel, the Salvation of Israel, laid the cornerstones for a synagogue. Designed by Peter Harrison, the brilliant colonial architect, who also drew the plans for King's Chapel in Boston, the synagogue was consecrated in 1763. Ezra Stiles, the Congregationalist minister in Newport at the time, called it one of the most perfect church buildings in America. The Reverend Stiles, later to become president of Yale College,

Touro Synagogue in Newport, not only an architectural gem and
a historic landmark but the oldest existing synagogue in the
United States. (*American Jewish Archives, Cincinnati*)

was throughout his career a friend to the Children of the Bible.

The Newport synagogue, a visible testament to the wealth and good taste of Newport's Jews, is the oldest and most charming synagogue still to be seen in this country. This house of worship, now called the Touro Synagogue, has become, under the terms of an act of Congress, a national historic shrine. Its hallowed burial ground, much older than the synagogue itself, prompted the poet Henry Wadsworth Longfellow to write:

*How strange it seems! These Hebrews in their
    graves,
    Close by the street of this fair seaport town,
Silent beside the never-silent waves,
    At rest in all this moving up and down! . . .*

*Gone are the living, but the dead remain
    And not neglected; for a hand unseen,
Scattering its bounty, like a summer rain,
    Still keeps their graves and their
        remembrance green.*

In 1761, two years after the synagogue cornerstones had been laid, the Jewish club of Newport was formed. The first of its kind in the United States, it was modeled after the social clubs of London, such as White's or Boodle's. Convivial evenings for men had as their centerpiece an elaborate meal with formal toasts, liberal allowances of drinks, animated conversation, and card games. Such was the urbanity of the great Jewish merchants of Newport that the amenities of their club equaled those to be enjoyed in Boston.

Some of the notable founders of the club were Naphtali Hart, Jacob Rodriguez Rivera, Isaac Polock, and Jacob Isaacs. Conspicuous by its absence is the name of Aaron Lopez, who was to become Newport's greatest merchant shipper and, according to Ezra Stiles, a preeminent merchant of colonial America. He was too poor to join the club at its founding.

Lopez was born in Portugal, the son of Diego Jose Lopez, a Marrano who secretly practiced Judaism while publicly professing Chris-

Aaron Lopez of Newport, an outstanding American patriot. He lost his fleet and his fortune in the revolutionary cause for freedom. (*American Jewish Archives, Cincinnati*)

Jacob Rodriguez Rivera, the most prominent of Newport's colonial Jews and a merchant shipper of wealth and culture. His son-in-law was the great Aaron Lopez. (*American Jewish Historical Society, Waltham, Mass.*)

tianity. Baptized Duarte, young Aaron witnessed the burning of Jewish heretics and vowed to flee Portugal for a land that offered some degree of religious liberty. His opportunity came in 1725, when his older half brother Moses invited him to Newport. With his wife and family the twenty-one-year-old Aaron vanished from Lisbon, surfacing in Newport several months later.

In America he was an open and pious Jew and a very energetic member of Newport's Congregation Jeshuat Israel; although a merchant of modest means at that time, he was accorded the singular honor of laying the first cornerstone for Newport's synagogue. For years he struggled to get ahead, but with little capital came little success. In 1762 Abigail, his loyal companion from the desperate days in Lisbon, died; they had had seven children, most of whom died young, a not unusual circumstance in colonial times.

For his second wife he chose Sarah, the daughter of Jacob Rodriguez Rivera, a charter member of the Jewish club and one of Newport's richest merchants. With that marriage the fortunes of Aaron Lopez took a phenomenal rise. Within five years he owned, in whole or in part, 30 oceangoing vessels and more than 100 coastal schooners. His ships and trade were known from Newfoundland to the West Indies, from Lisbon to London, and throughout the American colonial ports. His father-in-law, Jacob Rivera, shared in many of Lopez's enterprises, including the making of sperm oil candles, which revolutionized colonial lighting.

Lopez, despite his power and wealth, never forgot the sufferings of his youth and was judged by those who knew him to be a gentleman of charm and genuine humility. Ezra Stiles wrote of him: "Without a single Enemy and the most universally beloved by an extensive acquaintance of any man I ever knew."

During the Revolution Lopez suffered grievously, along with other Newport Jews who fervently backed the patriot cause with blood and treasure. His fleet fell into the hands of the British and remained there. When the British occupied Newport, he fled with others to Leicester, Massachusetts, where they formed the first Jewish settlement in that colony.

Rabbi Isaac Carigal, the scholar from Hebron in Palestine, who arrived in Newport in 1773 and became a close friend of the Reverend Ezra Stiles. (*American Jewish Archives, Cincinnati*)

Isaac Touro, cited in Newport's colonial records as "Parson Tororo Jew Priest," was the first rabbi of Newport's synagogue and the father of Judah Touro, one of America's greatest philanthropists. (*American Jewish Archives, Cincinnati*)

Parson Ezra Stiles of Newport, one of the most learned ministers in colonial America. He was a student of the Old Testament and an admirer of the children of Abraham. (*American Jewish Archives, Cincinnati*)

Lopez, nearly insolvent, died in 1782 and was buried in Newport's Jewish cemetery. In his will he gave a liberal contribution to Newport's now-famous Redwood Library, among other philanthropic gifts. The patriotic Lopez, brilliant and energetic, lost much for love of country, adopted as it was.

The Touros were an ancient Dutch Jewish family who had settled in Curaçao as early as 1650. Isaac Touro, at the age of twenty, settled in Newport and, while a merchant, became the first rabbi of its synagogue. In the early days of the Revolution Rabbi Isaac Touro was accused of being a Tory, which he probably was; he was cited in Newport's court records as "Parson Tororo Jew Priest"—a fine example of colonial misstatement, to say nothing of colonial taste. Forced to flee, he and his wife, Reyna Hays, and their two small sons, Judah and

Abraham, escaped to Kingston, Jamaica, where Rabbi Touro died. Moses Michael Hays, the eminent Boston merchant and brother to the widowed Reyna, brought her and the two boys to Boston, where the children were reared as members of his household.

Judah and Abraham Touro, now grown to manhood, became enormously wealthy, Judah as the leading trader of New Orleans and Abraham, one of Boston's most prominent merchant shippers. In remembrance of their father, Isaac, Judah and Abraham Touro contributed more than $20,000 to the preservation of Newport's synagogue, which had been closed since about 1800. This was a munificent gift, and the synagogue was reopened in 1850, with the Newport recollection that "the synagogue, the street on which it is situated, as also the burying grounds, are kept in elegant order, from the

Yale College in colonial times. Ezra Stiles was to become its president. (*The New York Public Library*)

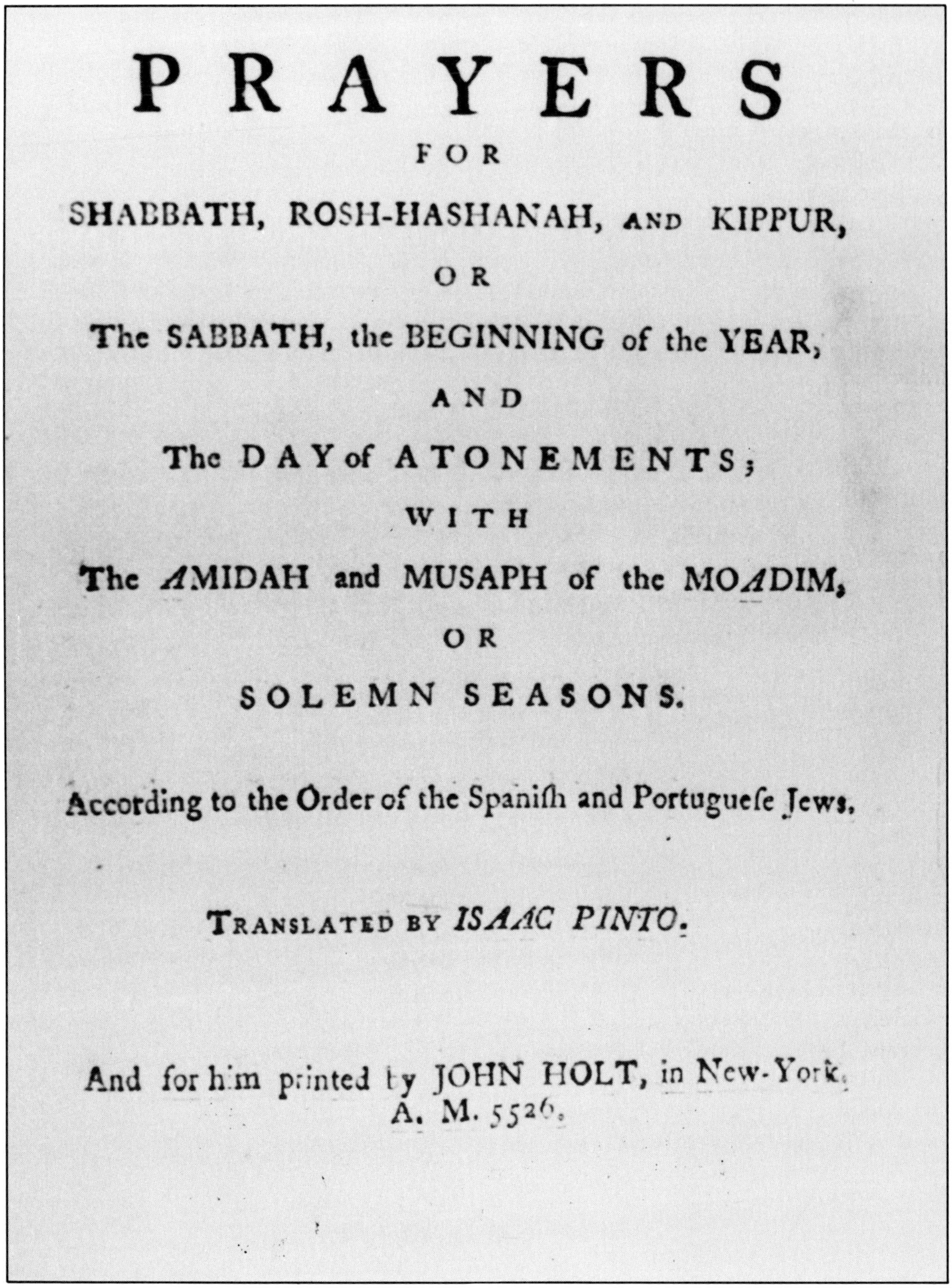

PRAYERS

FOR

SHABBATH, ROSH-HASHANAH, AND KIPPUR,

OR

The SABBATH, the BEGINNING of the YEAR,

AND

The DAY of ATONEMENTS;

WITH

The AMIDAH and MUSAPH of the MOADIM,

OR

SOLEMN SEASONS.

According to the Order of the Spanish and Portuguese Jews.

TRANSLATED BY ISAAC PINTO.

And for him printed by JOHN HOLT, in New-York.
A. M. 5526.

Title page from the first Jewish prayer book issued in America in a language other than Hebrew; the date given is 1766. Isaac Pinto, its translator, was the first in a long line of American Jewish publishers in New York City. (*American Jewish Archives, Cincinnati*)

proceeds of a legacy by the late Abraham Touro, now amounting to fifteen thousand dollars, and to the liberality of the well known Judah Touro of New Orleans."

Under the spurring terms of the legacy, Rhode Island passed an auspicious law providing that neither the City Council of Newport or any other town should in any manner "interfere with or restrain the full free exercise of the Jewish religion in said synagogue by any individual of that faith residing in Newport."

Before we lower the curtain on Roger Williams's noble experiment in Rhode Island, our attention should be drawn to one of those wandering Hebrew scholars who, from time to time, stayed for a brief visit in Newport, rested awhile, collected some money, and then wandered on. In 1773 Rabbi Isaac Carigal, a Jew of great learning from distant Hebron in Palestine, arrived in Newport. He had spent nearly twenty years in the quest for funds for the Jewish poor of Palestine. During the few months this exotic bird of passage remained in Newport he struck up a close friendship with the Reverend Ezra Stiles. The parson, one of the most erudite Americans of his day, spoke many languages, including Hebrew, and he and the rabbi spent long hours in deep discussion of the Holy Land, the Bible, and the Talmud. After the rabbi had left Newport, the two kept up a correspondence in Hebrew, Spanish, and English, until Carigal died in Barbados, still raising money for his people.

Years later, as president of Yale and professor of Hebrew, Stiles admonished his young scholars to study the Hebrew Psalms, for these "would be the first we should hear sung in heaven, and that he would be ashamed that any one of his pupils should be entirely ignorant of that holy language."

In 1781 Stiles, writing to influential Newport Jews, asked that an oil portrait of his friend the late Rabbi Carigal be presented to Yale College, suggesting that "it would be honorable to your nation as well as ornamental to this university." Samuel King, a Newport artist, who had met Carigal, was duly commissioned by old Jacob Rivera and others. The proud painting was delivered and hung "in the Publick Library of Yale College."

British and American depredations during the Revolutionary War had so weakened Newport that at its close the city declined as a major American port. Sea trade had shifted, and the glitter and riches of former days were gone. By the early 1800s the Jewish merchant princes had virtually vanished, perhaps to Boston, New York, Philadelphia or elsewhere. In the late nineteenth century new life was brought to Newport by the tycoons and magnates of the gentile superrich, who turned the city into a summer playground. Its Jewish heritage remains as a haunting memory to poets and to others who care.

Conspicuous as Jews were in the life of the thirteen colonies, they probably numbered fewer than 6,000 prior to the American Revolution. Success, achievement, and social visibility, gifts that were to serve them well—and badly—seemed to come their way in the ensuing decades. Mark Twain, the wise raconteur, once remarked perceptively, "Jews were like anyone else, only more so."

From the crucible of colonial hardship was to emerge a new kind of Jew: the American Jew, pilgrim and pioneer, settler and patriot.

VALLEY FORGE

E PLURIBUS UNUM

PART THREE

◄ Valley Forge in the desperate winter of 1777–1778. Jewish patriots suffered with their gentile comrades-in-arms. (*American Jewish Archives, Cincinnati*)

Settlers and Patriots

IN THE OLD WORLD the pious Jew, whatever his occupation, studied religious literature, pondered the fate of his people, and prayed for the coming of the Messiah. Rocking back and forth, he exulted in the Jewish martyrs who had died for the glorification of His Name. Here, in colonial towns, in the midst of the primeval forest, on this vast continent, the pioneer Jew, who had to face hostile Indians and dare the hazards of frontier life, was surely not the same man who, vilified by his Christian masters, silently intoned the Talmud in the dismal ghettos of Europe. From the days of Peter Stuyvesant a new man, a new Jew, free from ghetto humiliations, had arisen on the American landscape. The ancient Jew with the long white beard, the skullcap, the curling sideburns, the bent head, the downtrodden stereotypical Jew was largely the creation of antisemitic Europe.

In the early days of the Massachusetts Bay colony and elsewhere in New England, practicing Jews were not made welcome. Dominated by Puritan theocrats—those anointed champions of God—New England treated dissenters and apostates harshly. Led by Cotton Mather and, before him, his father, Increase Mather, the Puritan hierarchy aggressively fought religious error. Learned educators were these Pilgrim fathers: Increase was to become president of Harvard College, while his son was one of the moving spirits in the founding of Yale.

Cotton Mather, quite a different kind of minister from the great Ezra Stiles, was tireless in his efforts to convert the Jews.

Smug, self-righteous, fascinated, and even obsessed by the descendants of the ancient Hebrews, the Boston pastor wrote voluminously, proving, to his own satisfaction at least, that if the Jews would only return to the study of the Old Testament, they would see the errors of their ways and embrace Christianity. Actually Jews had never left the study of their Holy Scriptures, but Parson Mather, who was to die in 1728, fancied himself the sole source of revealed religion in the colonies.

Puritan theology, steeped as it was in the Hebrew Scriptures, literally reflected the words of biblical prophecy that soon after the Jews had been dispersed throughout the lands of the earth, there was to be a calling together of the Jewish nation, its conversion to the message of the Messiah would follow, and then the millennium would come. Without this fantasy event the kingdom of God could not be established on earth. New England clerics, supported by their congregations, had little or no use for Jews, who would not accept Jesus as the Messiah. Frustrated as they were, New Englanders of that period were determined to establish their own Canaan in America without the stiff-necked Jews. One wonders at times if the Puritans did not cherish thoughts of themselves as the true Chosen People and Jews merely an accident of history.

The Pulitzer Prize historian James Truslow Adams wrote penetratingly of the Puritans: "In spirit they may be considered as Jews and not Christians. Their God was the God of the Old Testament, their laws were the laws of the Old Testament, their guides to conduct were the characters of the Old Testament." The teaching of Hebrew, the sacred language, was often mandatory in the schools of early New England.

A revealing New England success story was that of Judah Monis. This scholarly Jew, of Spanish or Portuguese descent, had arrived prior to 1716, in New York, where he composed an instruction book for the study of Hebrew. In 1720, residing in Boston, he sent it to the worthies of Harvard College, who in the same year, encouraged by an interested group of Puritan divines, conferred the degree of Master

Cotton Mather of the Massachusetts Bay colony, the most erudite bigot of his time. (*The New York Public Library*)

of Arts on Monis for his Hebrew grammar; he thus became the first Jew in America to receive a degree from any college, and it was a Harvard degree.

As Monis must have suspected, his ministerial sponsors sought his conversion. Two years later, in March 1722, Monis accepted conversion in ceremonies at Harvard College itself; the following month he was appointed instructor in Hebrew, a post he held until his retirement in 1760. In the intervening years Monis conducted himself as a pious and upright Christian, except for the Sabbath, which he always observed on Saturday. His Hebrew grammar, finally printed with aid from the college in 1735, was the first Hebrew book published in North America. Judah Monis is to be remembered as Harvard's first house Jew.

The dour Puritans constructed a rigid union of church and state that was to be the envy of other would-be religious colonies. Dissenters themselves, the Puritans abhorred other dissenters and Jews. Jews nonetheless wandered in and out of the colony from 1649 on, as court records indicate. One such, named Solomon, was prosecuted in 1668 for traveling through a Massachusetts village on a Sunday. The Sabbath was not to be broken, not even by George Washington himself, who in later years was arrested in Connecticut for traveling on the Lord's Day.

Jewish merchants began to arrive in Boston, a great American port, in the first decade of the 1700s. Quiet and circumspect, the early Jews of Boston were always in fear of being "warned out" of that center of Puritan life. Among the earliest of merchants was Joseph Frazon, a member of an illustrious Sephardic family, who died in Boston in 1704. In those days Boston Jews customarily went to Newport, New York, or Albany for marriage or burial; it was not until the 1730s or 1740s that a small Jewish burial ground appeared on the outskirts of the Pilgrim town. Judge Samuel Sewall, one of the most human of Puritans,

דקדוק לשון עברית

DICKDOOK LESHON GNEBREET.

A

GRAMMAR

OF THE

Hebrew Tongue,

BEING

An ESSAY

To bring the Hebrew Grammar into English,

to Facilitate the

INSTRUCTION

Of all those who are desirous of acquiring a clear Idea of this

Primitive Tongue

by their own Studies;

In order to their more distinct Acquaintance with the SACRED ORACLES of the Old Testament, according to the Original. And Published more especially for the Use of the STUDENTS of HARVARD-COLLEGE at *Cambridge*, in NEW-ENGLAND.

נחבר והוגה בעיון נמרץ על ידי
יהודה מוניש

Composed and accurately Corrected,

By JUDAH MONIS, M. A.

BOSTON, N. E.

Printed by JONAS GREEN, and are to be Sold by the AUTHOR at his House in *Cambridge*. MDCCXXXV.

The work that brought Judah Monis to the attention of the Puritan divines of Harvard College. Composed prior to 1720, this Hebrew grammar was to turn Monis into Harvard's first house Jew. (*American Jewish Historical Society, Waltham, Mass.*)

Harvard College as it looked to the Hebrew scholar Judah Monis in the eighteenth century. (*The New York Public Library*)

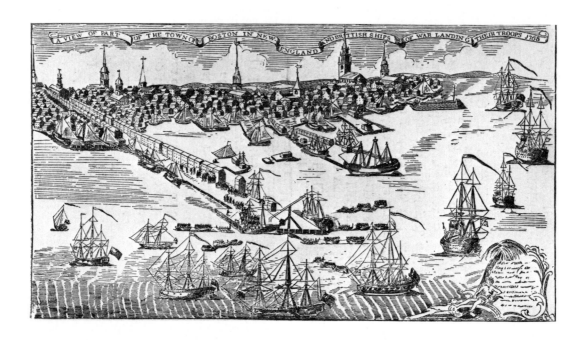

The British landing troops in colonial Boston, a city well known for its revolutionary fervor. (*The New York Public Library*)

Moses Michael Hays, the most prominent Jew in colonial Boston. (*American Jewish Archives, Cincinnati*)

noted in his diary: "Joseph Frazon, the Jew, dyes at Mr. Majors . . . Satterday, is carried in Simson's coach to Bristow, from thence by water to Newport where there is a Jews-burying place."

Religious intolerance for years prevented the formation of a Jewish congregation in Boston, but finally, in 1851, a synagogue was erected on Warrenton Street, one little temple among the sixty-eight churches of the city.

Moses Michael Hays, destined to become one of Boston's most prominent citizens and its leading Jewish businessman, was born in New York in 1739. A watchmaker by trade, he suffered years of hardship before moving to Newport. There, after having been imprisoned for debts, he enjoyed some modest success as a retail merchant. With the high political passions of 1776 Hays's loyalty to the American cause was impugned, a dangerous situation in those inflamed days. Rumor and suspicion arrayed neighbor against neighbor, family against family.

In postrevolutionary Boston, the cradle of American liberty, Jews were still excluded from the public worship of their religion. (*The New York Public Library*)

Rhode Island at that time of stress required an oath of loyalty from any male who was "suspected of being inimical to the United American Colonies and the arduous struggle in which they are engaged against the force of Great Britain." Hays was so accused and brought to court but, smarting under the injustice and indignity of having his loyalty challenged, refused to take the oath. He demanded to be confronted by his accusers, countered their empty charges, and in an eloquent plea firmly established his patriotism, which no one ever again questioned.

Business drew Hays to Boston, and there he finally found the good fortune that had for so long eluded him. Highly intelligent, he undertook marine insurance in the bustling port and from that branched into banking, the China trade, and real estate, becoming socially eminent even among the antisemitic Bostonians. In 1784, at age forty-five, Hays joined several gentile merchant bankers to form the Massachusetts Bank, now the First National Bank of Boston, one of the largest banks in the country. The influential Hays, champion of cultural and social causes, played a leading role in the reopening of theater in Boston after it had been banned as a source of frivolity and immorality. Gaiety was never a puritanical strongpoint.

From 1788 on Hays was grand master of the Grand Lodge of Masons in Massachusetts; his deputy was Paul Revere. Hays was known for his many kind attentions to the poor, Jew and gentile alike. He was the affluent uncle who reared his penniless nephews, the brothers Touro. This American tycoon was the first Jewish benefactor of Harvard College.

On the death of Moses Michael Hays in 1805 the *Boston Centinel* wrote: "He walked abroad *fearing* no man, but *loving* all. He was without guile, detesting hypocrisy as a despised meanness! Take him for all in all, he was indeed a man."

JEWISH PEDDLERS AND TRADERS had done business in the Connecticut river towns since 1659 but fared no better there than in neighboring Massachusetts. Jews who tried to settle in Hartford did not remain long, and in New London Jewish ship cargo was arbitrarily seized. Very much a part of Puritan New England, Connecticut treated Jews at best as aliens; at worst they were faithless heathens "whose nation sold their God for money and crucified him afterwards." While Jewish communal life was impossible in Connecticut in those days, individual Jewish families were to be found in many of the larger towns. The Pintos, for example, had been settled in Stratford since 1725. Other towns that sheltered Jews were Stamford, Norwalk, Wilton, and Danbury.

Settled for a time in Wilton was the aged Joseph Simson, a passionate patriot who had fled New York in the face of British harassment. A German Jew, he arrived in Manhattan in 1718. His sons Sampson and Solomon became wealthy New York merchants; it was Solomon

Ohebei Shalom was the first Jewish congregation allowed to build a synagogue in the city of Boston, and a small temple was opened in 1851. (*American Jewish Archives, Cincinnati*)

Joseph Simson, the German Jew who arrived in Manhattan in 1718. A passionate patriot, he fled New York in the face of British harassment and settled in Wilton, Connecticut, where he supported the American cause. (*American Jewish Archives, Cincinnati*)

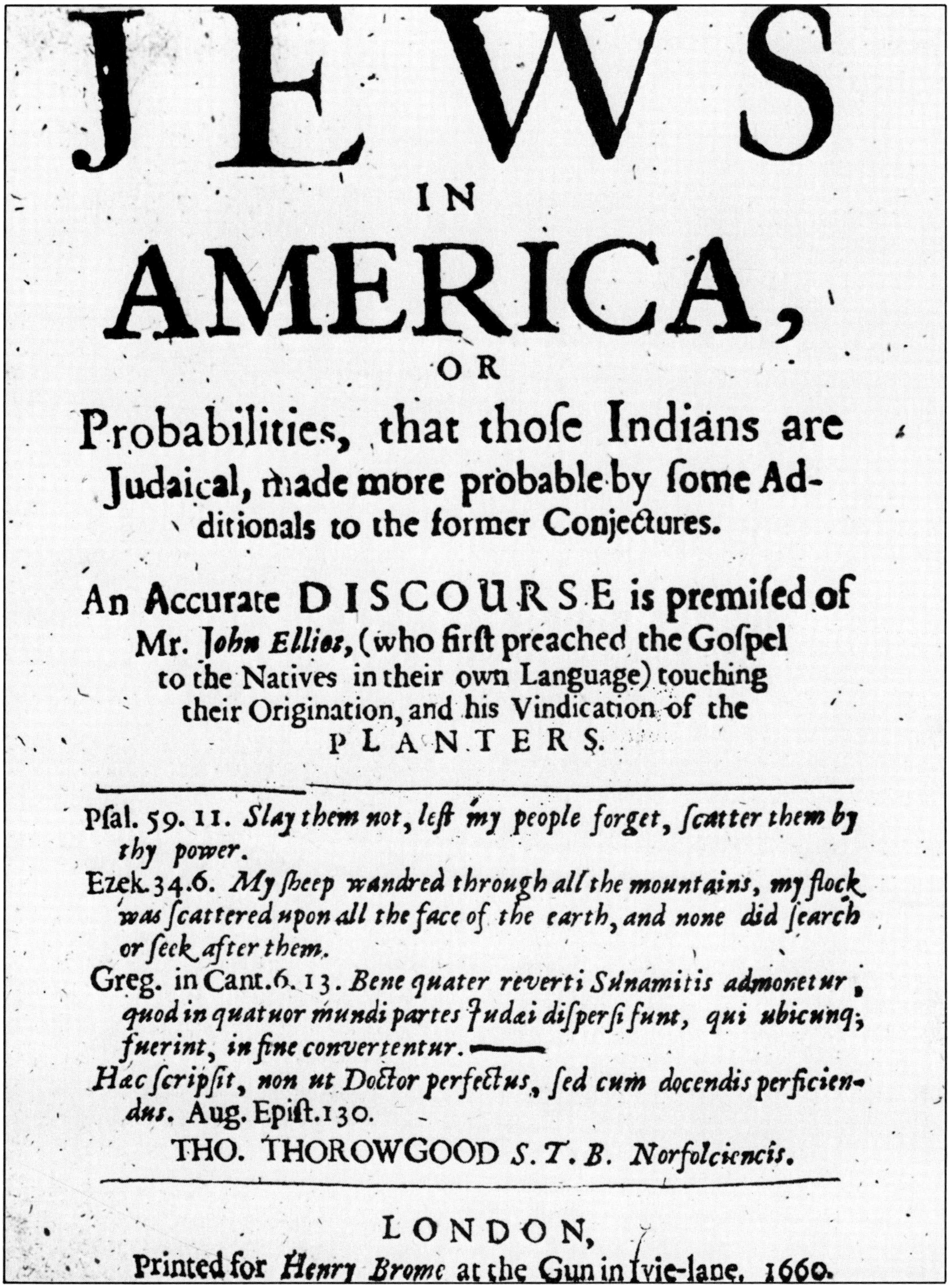

JEWS

IN

AMERICA,

OR

Probabilities, that thofe Indians are Judaical, made more probable by fome Additionals to the former Conjectures.

An Accurate DISCOURSE is premifed of Mr. *John Ellios*, (who firft preached the Gofpel to the Natives in their own Language) touching their Origination, and his Vindication of the PLANTERS.

Pfal. 59. 11. *Slay them not, left my people forget, fcatter them by thy power.*

Ezek. 34.6. *My fheep wandred through all the mountains, my flock was fcattered upon all the face of the earth, and none did fearch or feek after them.*

Greg. in Cant.6. 13. *Bene quater reverti Sunamitis admonetur, quod in quatuor mundi partes Judai difperfi funt, qui ubicunq; fuerint, in fine convertentur.* ——

Hac fcripfit, non ut Doctor perfectus, fed cum docendis perficiendus. Aug. Epift.130.

THO. THOROWGOOD *S. T. B. Norfolciencis.*

LONDON,

Printed for *Henry Brome* at the Gun in Ivie-lane. 1660.

The titlepage of the book that promoted the fallacy that the American Indians were really the ten lost tribes of Israel. John Eliot, the famous Puritan missionary, was so enchanted with the idea that he often preached sermons to the Indian tribes of New England in Hebrew. (*American Jewish Archives, Cincinnati*)

Simson who formulated a plan for the new United States Mint. Old Joseph Simson taught patriotism to all who would listen, for although an octogenarian, he vividly recalled the yellow "Jew badge" he was forced to wear in Germany and the misery of the Frankfurt ghetto.

A learned Hebraist, he was sought after by scholars from Oxford and Columbia, and even Ezra Stiles called on him. Sampson Simson, grandson of the grand old man, was graduated from Columbia College in 1800, was a veteran of the War of 1812, and became a founder of Mount Sinai Hospital in Manhattan.

In patriotic Norwalk, Connecticut, was Michael Judah, a merchant who had been settled there since the 1740s. A loyal and observant Jew, he left his small estate to Jewish widows and orphans. His son David fought in the Connecticut line during the Revolution. Another early Jew in the Fairfield area was Anshil Troib, who, after trying earnestly to maintain his Jewishness in the midst of gentile hostility, died as Andris Trube and was given a Christian burial.

Before we leave colonial New England, a limited discourse on the ten lost tribes of Israel might be appropriate. Among serious Christians of yesterday and the Bible-Belters of today, a daily reading of the Lord's Book was and is required. The words of biblical prophecy, metaphoric as they may sometimes seem, were and are to be taken literally.

When Sargon II of Assyria conquered the northern kingdom of the ancient Hebrews in about 721 B.C. he deported the people of the Book en masse. According to the Bible, until these lost tribes of Israelites are found and brought to a great convocation of all the Jewish tribes, there can be no millennium. Within the logic of the prophecy it became necessary to uncover the lost tribes, who were probably hiding, awaiting the Lord's call. The search took many curious and odd turns in early Christendom, and for several centuries the puzzle of the lost tribes was one of the most popular mysteries of Europe.

In 1650 the Reverend Thomas Thorowgood of England published a book entitled *Jews in America, or Probabilities That the Americans Are of That Race.* It proved that at long last and be-

yond doubt, the American Indians were the ten lost tribes of Israelites. This was not an original discovery since as early as 1585 a Catholic priest, in a history of New Spain, drew the same conclusion from the fancied resemblance between so-called Jewish rites and those of the Mexican Indians. The Thorowgood book, staunchly Puritan in tone and style, received the official approval of the London censors, the English government being under the control of the Puritan hierarchy at the time. Funds from its sale were sent to the young John Eliot, the Apostle to the Indians, who was then preaching the Gospel to the Indians of the Massachusetts colony.

Moses Seixas, a banker in eighteenth-century Newport. The Sephardic Seixas family was among the most prominent in colonial America.
(*American Jewish Archives, Cincinnati*)

Gershom Mendes Seixas, born in New York in 1746, was America's first native-born rabbi and for years the chief spokesman of American Jewry. The leader of Congregation Shearith Israel, he was also active with the Minutemen and in later years was elected trustee of Columbia College. (*American Jewish Archives, Cincinnati*)

Columbia College as it looked to Rabbi Gershom Mendes Seixas. (*The New York Public Library*)

Menasseh ben Israel, a distinguished rabbi in Amsterdam, impressed with the popularity of the Thorowgood polemic, decided to provoke an interview with Oliver Cromwell, the Lord Protector of England. Perhaps, he thought, this theory of the Indians being Jews could be used for the benefit of real Jews: There had been a ban against the admission of Jews to England since 1290. In a pamphlet addressed *To the Parliament, the Supreme Court of England,* the shrewd rabbi promoted the Jewish origins of the Indians and even supplied testimony by one Antonio de Montezinos, a Portuguese Jew, who said he had witnessed Jewish ceremonies among the "savages" of South America. Cromwell, fascinated, agreed to meet with Menasseh, who convinced the Lord Protector that it was in England's best interest to readmit the Jews; this was done quietly and without molestation. In America the Thorowgood thesis was foolishly argued and reargued well into the nineteenth century, proving once again the stamina of a meretricious fallacy.

John Myers of Norfolk, Virginia, merchant and patriot. (*American Jewish Archives, Cincinnati*)

PRIOR TO AND AFTER the American Revolution, New York was the heartland of American Jewry. Among the city's most eminent Jewish representatives was the Seixas family, with members in Newport, Philadelphia, and Charleston. The founder of this remarkable clan was Isaac Mendes Seixas, who fled Portugal and arrived in New York via Barbados in about 1734. A young immigrant merchant, he courted and married Rachel Levy, who was not only a Levy but a Franks. Stormy scenes marred the courtship since the Levys and Frankses, wealthy and established Ashkenazic families, resented the pretensions and arrogance of Sephardic Jews. While it is true that the Sephardics, first arrivals in America, lorded it over the Dutch and German Jews, it is also true that the German Jews followed suit against the later Polish and East European immigrants; the social wheel continues to turn, and when, if ever, Oriental Jews are admitted to the United States, the East Europeans will assert their right of domain.

Isaac and Rachel Levy Seixas lived in New York until the late 1740s, when they moved to Newport. Among their several children born in New York and Newport were Abraham Seixas, who fought as a Revolutionary officer in Georgia and South Carolina but spent most of his mature years as a Charleston merchant; Moses Seixas, one of the organizers of the Bank of Rhode Island; Benjamin Seixas, one of the founders of the New York Stock Exchange; and Gershom Mendes Seixas, the Patriot Rabbi.

The Myers Mansion in Norfolk, Virginia, the home of John Myers.
(*American Jewish Archives, Cincinnati*)

The interior of the famous Charleston synagogue, as depicted by the American Jewish artist Solomon Carvalho, in the early nineteenth century. (*American Jewish Archives, Cincinnati*)

Gershom Seixas, born in New York in 1746, was to become America's first native-born rabbi and for years the chief spokesman of American Jewry. At age twenty-two, this handsome, charming, and intelligent young man was elected the spiritual leader of Congregation Shearith Israel in New York, an office he filled with distinction for the next forty-eight years. With roots firmly planted in American soil he was popular even among establishment gentiles. He was paid little; his congregation upheld the time-honored belief that clergymen should be not only humble but

poor. Seixas was the first rabbi to preach a sermon in English in an American synagogue.

Active with the Minutemen, the young Seixas delivered his first patriotic sermon in August 1776. When the British struck at New York during the Revolution, the rabbi and other Jews fled first to nearby Connecticut and from there to Philadelphia, which had become a haven for refugee patriots. In the Quaker city, a hotbed of seditious Americanism, Seixas and his fellow New Yorkers helped bring new life to the members of Congregation Mikveh Israel, among whom were the Gratz family and Haym

Solomon. Seixas returned to New York and the Mill Street Synagogue in 1784.

For years Gershom Mendes Seixas was repeatedly honored as an American patriot and citizen. He was often invited to speak at churches; a rabbi preaching to Christian congregations was very unusual for the time. In 1784 the Reverend Seixas, for so he was called, was elected a regent and trustee of Columbia College, an institution he faithfully served for thirty years. As a tribute to his memory Columbia, on its 175th anniversary, unveiled a painting of the highly respected Seixas. It is said that Rabbi Seixas was one of the fourteen clergymen who officiated at George Washington's inauguration in 1789. Seixas was the first in a long and distinguished line of American-born rabbis.

Abraham Isaac Abrahams, a New York Jew of Lithuanian descent, was the most fashionable circumciser, or *mohel,* in the colonies. He traveled widely his duty to perform. Abrahams began to chronicle his work as a *mohel* in 1756, and his first recorded circumcision was that of his own son Isaac, who in 1774 became the first Jewish graduate of King's (now Columbia) College. His background notwithstanding, Isaac Abrahams chose to become a surgeon rather than the rabbi his father hoped he would be.

One of the most appreciated artisans of the period was Myer Myers. A master silversmith, Myers was born in New York in 1723, the scion of a large Dutch Jewish family. His highly valued work is famous for its rich design and exquisite ornamentation and may be seen in museums, synagogues, churches, and major private collections. Among the most gifted of colonial silversmiths, Myers may be considered the first of many American-born Jewish artists. In 1786 he was elected president of the gentile and prestigious Silversmiths' Guild of New York. Active in synagogue affairs, he was for several years the president of Congregation Shearith Israel.

Samuel Myers, son of the famous silversmith, served in the Virginia line during the Revolution. He became a partner in the firm of Isaac Moses and Company, which acquired great wealth by daring to run the British block-

Isaac Harby, an educator, journalist, and dramatist, was born to the Harbys of Charleston in 1788. An active American Jew, he corresponded with Thomas Jefferson. Silhouette portraits were considered elegant at the time. (*American Jewish Archives, Cincinnati*)

ade of the 1770s. After the war Myers settled in Virginia, first in Petersburg, then in Norfolk, and finally in Richmond, where by 1800 he was a well-known merchant. The genealogy of the Myers clan is unclear, but among its members were: Benjamin Myers, the first-known Jew in Nashville, arriving before 1795; John Myers, Norfolk merchant and veteran of the War of 1812; Levy Myers, physician and South Carolina state legislator in 1796; Mordecai Myers, of Georgetown, South Carolina, who was a leading purveyor of military supplies to Francis Marion, the Swamp Fox, during the Revolution; and Moses Myers, a major in the

Virginia militia, who became superintendent of the Norfolk Bank of Richmond.

Another Jewish artist of the Myers period was Joshua Canter, who appeared in Charleston in 1792 and taught drawing and painting there; little is known of his life. In the same city years before lived David Lopez, who, it is said, was the Jewish builder and architect of the synagogue Beth Elohim, the House of God, in 1750. The congregation is among the three or four oldest in North America.

Southern gentry, prosperous and social, were the colonial Jews of Charleston. Plantation owners, merchants, and, sad to say, slave dealers, these Charlestonians began to arrive in South Carolina in the 1690s, under the liberal terms of John Locke's colonial charter. Sephardic and Ashkenazic names grace the beginning pages of the history of that charming port city; Lindo, De la Motta, Lopez, Cardozo, Salvador, Harby, Moise, and Cohen were to become commonplace.

Moses Lindo, who helped create the indigo dye industry in the colonies, settled in Charleston in 1756, after having spent several years in England. Of Portuguese descent, with large financial reserves, he established a great plantation near Charleston to grow the indigo plant, from which is produced the valuable dye now called Carolina blue. In constant touch with the chemists of London's Royal Society, Lindo promoted the fabulous Carolina indigo trade which was largely responsible for the colony's wealth. It was his mark of inspection, and only his mark, that certified Carolina-grown indigo in British markets. Lindo, because of his efforts on behalf of the British crown, was awarded the right to display the royal coat of arms, and he often did.

Wealthy merchant and planter, Lindo was a benefactor of Rhode Island College (now Brown University) in Providence. This eminent Charlestonian was familiar with the Jewish exclusionary policies of English universities and must have appreciated the generous words of the Rhode Island College resolution that read: "Voted that the children of the Jews may be admitted into this institution and enjoy the

It was Thomas Jefferson, the brilliant Virginian, who commented on intolerance thus: "Public opinion erects itself into an Inquisition, and exercises its office with as much fanaticism as fans the flames of an Auto da fe." (*The New York Public Library*)

freedom of their religion, without any restraint or imposition whatsoever."

Another Charlestonian Jew of renown was Francis Salvador. Colorful plantation owner and courageous patriot, Salvador won the fanciful epithet of the Southern Paul Revere. This brilliant young English Jew of Portuguese ancestry arrived in Charleston in 1773 to oversee and develop his family's large landholdings there. Within a year, an ardent patriot and influential landowner, he joined Charles Pinckney and Edward Rutledge in the Provincial Congress of South Carolina. Less than a month after the promulgation of the Declaration of Independence, Salvador, an officer in the Caro-

Abraham Moise, the founder of the Moise clan of Charleston and the father of Penina Moise. (*American Jewish Archives, Cincinnati*)

lina militia, was ambushed, scalped, and killed by the British-backed Cherokee Indians while on patrol. He was twenty-nine years old. Patriot, legislator, and soldier, he was the first of the many American Jews to give his life for his country.

A memorial plaque dedicated to Francis Salvador in Charleston reads in part: "Born an aristocrat, he became a democrat; an Englishman, he cast his lot with America; true to his ancient faith, he gave his life for new hopes of human liberty and understanding."

The Harby family, one of the most outstanding of early American Jewish families, was founded by Solomon Harby, who arrived in Charleston after 1781. Among his many children were George Washington Harby, who was a Charleston playwright; Henry Jefferson Harby, active in Carolina politics; Levy Myers Harby, who fought in the War of 1812 and commanded a Confederate ship in the Civil War; and Isaac Harby, perhaps the most illustrious of the well-to-do and cultivated Charleston clan.

Isaac Harby, born in 1788, was an educator, journalist, and dramatist, who wrote his first play at the age of seventeen. He established schools in Charleston, was the editor of the *Southern Patriot,* among other journals, and was a founder of the Reformed Society of Israelites, which was the forerunner of the Jewish Reform movement in America. In response to a letter from Harby, Thomas Jefferson forcefully stated his position that sectarian influences should be eliminated from public education, and to that end, he wrote, he was playing a prominent role in the founding of the University of Virginia. This, of course, pleased Harby, who was deeply concerned with unsympathetic religious influences on Jewish students seeking public education.

Another Charleston family was the Moises. Its founder, Abraham Moise, was of French origin and first came to notice as a Charleston merchant in 1791. Aaron Moise, his son, was a physician; another son, Abraham, was an outstanding attorney and Carolina politician; Jacob, another member of the brood, was among the earliest Jewish settlers of Augusta,

View of Charleston at the time of Penina Moise. (*The New York Public Library*)

Georgia, and became a director of the Georgia Insurance Company; and then there was Penina, the greatest of the Moises.

Penina Moise, daughter of old Abraham, was born in Charleston in 1797. Until she was twelve, she led a comfortable life as the daughter of a Charleston merchant. However, after her father died the family of nine children slipped to near poverty. Her mother, Sarah, became first ill and finally paralyzed, and the young Penina was forced to leave school to care for the house and her invalid mother. The older children found work to help support the family, as did Penina, who made lace and embroidery for the rich of Charleston. Later she earned her livelihood as a schoolteacher.

While still in her teens, this remarkable girl, the pillar of her family, showed poetic gifts. Self-taught, a voracious reader, and deeply concerned with her people, she would compose even by moonlight if she could be spared from household duties. She wrote stirring poetry, which, much to her surprise, was published by the *Charleston Courier* on a regular basis. By 1830 her poetry and prose appeared in the leading journals of the time, and in 1835 she became widely known and discussed with the publication of her volume of verses *Fancy's Sketch Book.* The poor Jewish maiden, too proud to ask for help, was lionized by the literary folk of Charleston, to the pleasure and delight of the whole Moise family. Her native city regarded her as its poet laureate.

Penina, in later life, wrote synagogue hymns in English, which bring solace to the many who still sing them. Her volume of collected Jewish hymns is famous, and no other poet has more verses in the hymnal of the Union of American Hebrew Congregations than Penina Moise. She bore poverty and ill health with fortitude and grace, and in the last fifteen years of her life she was completely blind. This sweet and gracious lady, for years one of the much admired centers of Charleston's literary life, died a spinster at eighty-three. She leaves a remembrance of herself in the hymnal stanza:

For with unbroken trust will I
In Thee, my God, confide,
Who deigns the meek to dignify,
The arrogant to chide.

Of Central and East European descent were the many Cohens of colonial New York, Philadelphia, Baltimore, Richmond, and Savannah. In Charleston were Mordecai Cohen, a wealthy planter and philanthropist, who was commissioner of markets for the Southern port city; Gershom Cohen, a merchant and veteran of the Revolutionary War; his son Hyam Cohen, a hero of the War of 1812; Jacob Cohen, a silversmith who, during the Revolution, led a company of cavalry in Virginia; and the scandalous Cornelia Cohen, who in 1799 married a Thomas McIntyre in a Charleston church.

THE COLONY OF GEORGIA and its chief town, Savannah, were founded by James Oglethorpe, an English general and philanthropist and an aristocrat of generous spirit. Deeply concerned with the sufferings of the debtor classes of England, he decided to establish an asylum for debtors in America, which was to be called Georgia. This fitted in admirably with British military concern that a buffer colony be developed between Carolina and the Spanish then in Florida. Oglethorpe, leading 116 colonists, settled Savannah in February 1733. Largely as a result of the efforts of Oglethorpe himself, who probably felt that the children of Abraham were as deserving as his colony of debtors, Jews were admitted to Savannah within a few months of its founding. Then a village, Savannah, that hospitable Southern port, came to rival in charm and beauty the port of Charleston, its older sister city.

In the first shipload of Jewish colonists were the founders of the Minis, De Lyon (De Leon), Nunez, and Sheftall families. Abraham and Abigail Minis were among the first merchants of Georgia, and their son Philip, born in Savannah in July 1733, may have been the first white male child to be born in Georgia. He later served as commissary general and paymaster to the colonial militia during the Revolution. Abraham De Lyon, of Portuguese origin,

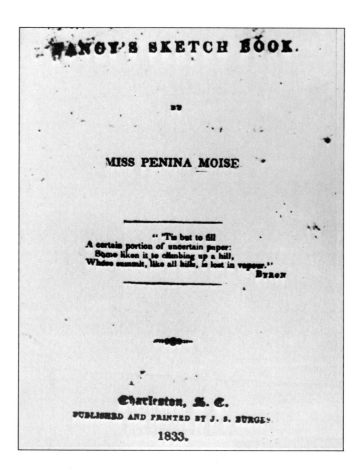

Titlepage of the work that made Miss Penina Moise the poet laureate of Charleston. (*American Jewish Archives, Cincinnati*)

was a planter in Savannah who pioneered wine growing in the colony. His grandson Abraham De Lyon, or De Leon, served as a surgeon with the Revolutionary forces.

Samuel Nunez, a Marrano who had been court physician in Portugal, arrived with his family in 1733 for a new life in Savannah. Apparently he came with wealth, for within a short time he had large landholdings in Georgia. Nonetheless, he continued to minister to the sick and poor of the colony. His son Moses Nunez was a large plantation owner, influential in early Georgia politics, who in later life married a Jewish mulatta. (In fairness to the Christian gentlemen of the Southland, Jews of the region were proportionately as active as they in the making of mulattoes.) Moses Nunez's

Mordecai Sheftall, the most famous of Savannah's Jews. He was a Revolutionary War hero, known to the British as "a very great rebel." (*American Jewish Archives, Cincinnati*)

The early nineteenth-century mansion of Abraham Tobias, Jewish merchant in Charleston. It is now a church. (*American Jewish Archives, Cincinnati*)

sister Zipporah, reared as a Catholic in Portugal, married David Mendez Machado, the cantor of Shearith Israel in New York. She became well known for her charity as well as for her cultivation.

The leading Jewish family of Savannah, and one of the most prominent in colonial Georgia, was the Sheftalls. The German Benjamin Sheftall landed in Savannah in 1733, along with the other first Jewish families of Georgia, and within a few years was an established planter. He was one of the founders of the Union Society of Savannah, a nonsectarian philanthropic organization, which was organized to unite Jew, Catholic, and Protestant for social betterment.

Among the planter's several children were Levi and Mordecai Sheftall. Levi, the younger brother, served in the Revolutionary army but was forced to flee Georgia for a while when he was unjustly suspected of Tory sympathies.

Mordecai, the most famous of the Sheftalls, was a prosperous plantation owner, rancher, and merchant in Savannah. An ardent patriot, he early opposed British rule in Georgia, and when the war broke out, he became the colonel of a militia brigade. Shortly thereafter he was appointed commissary general for the American forces in Georgia and South Carolina and became known to the British as "a very great rebel." His sixteen-year-old son, Sheftall Sheftall, was his deputy.

When the British captured Savannah in 1778, Mordecai and Sheftall Sheftall were taken

The Minis House in Savannah. The Minises, of Jewish origin, were among the first families of Georgia. (*American Jewish Archives, Cincinnati*)

prisoner after a brief engagement. Mordecai could have escaped, but his son was unable to swim. Ill-treated for several months on a British prison ship, often denied food, the Sheftalls were finally paroled to Sunbury, a small town in Georgia, where despite his being a prisoner of war, Mordecai Sheftall was elected president of the Union Society of Savannah. Soon after, however, father and son attempted an escape but were recaptured and exiled to the island of Antigua.

After the war the American government awarded Sheftall a land grant in recognition of his services to the patriot cause and as compensation in part for the money he had advanced for troop supplies, money never fully repaid. An observant Jew, this American hero became the driving force in the organization of Savannah Jewry.

Moses Sheftall, another son of the famous patriot, became a well-known physician and surgeon after studying under the great Dr. Ben-

jamin Rush, a signer of the Declaration of Independence. Moses was twice elected to the Georgia legislature. Jews held public office in Georgia even before revision of the oath of office, which included the words "upon the faith of a Christian." David Emanuel, a soldier of the Revolution, was elected governor of the state in 1801, the first Jewish governor of any state in the Union. However, it is most probable that long before he reached that political eminence, Emanuel had denied his own faith.

IN RICHMOND, the capital of Virginia, was Isaiah Isaacs, probably the first permanent Jewish settler in that town. By 1769 a silversmith, he soon became a prominent merchant dealing in goods, real estate, and slaves. His partner Jacob I. Cohen, who lived in Richmond from 1781, was a banker and land speculator. Isaacs and Cohen had business dealings with the great pathfinder Daniel Boone of Kentucky.

An existing gravestone in Savannah's Old Jewish Burial Ground. It is inscribed to Mordecai De Lyon, a leading light of Savannah's gentry. (*American Jewish Archives, Cincinnati*)

Plaque marking the site of the first Jewish cemetery in Georgia. Mordecai Sheftall, the revolutionary hero of Savannah, is mentioned prominently. (*American Jewish Archives, Cincinnati*)

OLD JEWISH BURIAL GROUND

Established by Mordecai Sheftall on August 2, 1773 from lands granted him in 1762 by King George III as a parcel of land that "shall be, and forever remain, to and for the use and purpose of a Place of Burial for all persons whatever professing the Jewish Religion."

During the ill fated attempt of the French forces under Admiral Charles Henri, Comte d'Estaing, and the American forces under General Benjamin Lincoln, to recapture Savannah from the British, General Lincoln's Orders of the Day of October 8, 1779 stated that "The second place of rallying, or the first if the redoubt should not be carried, will be at the Jew's burying ground, where the reserve will be placed."

According to the account of Captain Antoine-Françoise Térance O'Connor, a military engineer serving with the French forces, on October 9, 1779, shortly after 4:00 A.M. "The reserve corps, commanded by M. le Vicomte de Noailles, advanced as far as an old Jewish cemetery, and we placed on its right and a little to the rear the four 4-pounders."

Israel I. Cohen, the brother of Jacob, was a constable in Richmond and one of the founders of Congregation Beth Shalome, the House of Peace, some years prior to 1790. His son Philip served in the War of 1812 and later became postmaster of Norfolk, Virginia. Another Cohen of Richmond was Abraham Hyam Cohen, who is credited with having invented seltzer water and with promoting the use of soda pop in America.

Other Jews were Marcus Elcan, a wealthy merchant and leading citizen of Richmond, who possessed a fine library. Educated and well read, he was elected the first president of Congregation Beth Shalome. David Isaacs, who lived in Richmond for a while but settled in Charlottesville as a merchant in 1802, was a principal supporter of Thomas Jefferson in his efforts to establish a college in Virginia. There also were Aaron Cardozo, an English merchant who set up shop in Richmond, and Michael Israel, who fought in the Virginia militia against the Indians in 1758 but took up residence in Philadelphia. The Myers family of Virginia, closely related to the Myers family of New York, was mentioned earlier.

Richmond, fated to become the seat of the Confederacy, was to see the arrival of many Jews before the Civil War.

INHOSPITABLE WAS THE CLIMATE of colonial Maryland for "those deniers of Christ," the Jews. For those who settled there before the passage of the Jew Bill of 1825, which bestowed civil rights on the Jews, placing them "on the same footing with other good citizens," gentile hostility mixed with legal restrictions was an everyday fact of life. We have already noted the imprisonment of the "Jew doctor" Jacob Lumbrozo for blasphemy in seventeenth-century Maryland. In the mid-eighteenth century there was an Ansel Israells in the colony, and in 1773 a Benjamin Levy opened a dry goods store on Market Street in Baltimore. Another Benjamin Levy, the son of the great Moses Levy of New York, enjoyed social status in Baltimore as a prominent merchant and Indian trader. A friend of Robert Morris, he was involved early in patriotic activity.

Jacob I. Cohen of Richmond, the banker and land speculator who was in business with Daniel Boone of Kentucky. (*American Jewish Archives, Cincinnati*)

Another Maryland Jew of the period was Jacob Hart, a Bavarian who settled in Baltimore in 1775. A patriotic merchant, he advanced money to General Lafayette and supplied his soldiers with clothing and shoes. Nathaniel Levy, a member of the First Baltimore Cavalry, fought under Lafayette in the Revolution. And a Bela Israel was involved in a lawsuit in 1787 in Frederick County, Maryland, according to court records.

Two of the most illustrious Jewish families of early Baltimore were the Ettings and the Cohens. When Elijah Etting died in 1778 in York,

Hyman Marks, eighteenth-century Jewish merchant in Richmond. (*American Jewish Archives, Cincinnati*)

Beth Shalome in Richmond, Virginia. The congregation was founded prior to 1790. (*American Jewish Archives, Cincinnati*)

Pennsylvania, Shina Solomon Etting, his widow, moved with her five children to Baltimore. There she kept a boardinghouse on Market Street. A few years later her brothers Isaac, Myer, and Levi Solomon opened a hardware business in Baltimore.

Shina Etting's sons Reuben and Solomon became well-known and respected Baltimoreans. A soldier of the Revolutionary army, Reuben Etting was elected captain of Maryland's Independent Blues in 1788, and in 1801 he was appointed U.S. marshal for Maryland by President Jefferson. Etting came out of retirement to fight in the War of 1812. Solomon Etting, the younger brother, was one of the organizers and, for many years, a director of the Union Bank in Baltimore. An active proponent of the Jew Bill, he was elected to the City Council of Baltimore immediately after its passage; he was the first Jew to be elected to public office in Maryland. He later became president of the Council. One of the promoters of the Baltimore & Ohio Railroad, Solomon Etting also served on the first board of directors of that company.

Among Shina's grandchildren were Elijah Gratz Etting, a graduate of the University of Pennsylvania who became district attorney for Cecil County, Maryland; Henry Etting, who retired from the U.S. Navy with the rank of commodore; and Samuel Etting, who was wounded in the War of 1812.

Israel I. Cohen of Richmond was the father of the famous Cohen brothers, bankers and brokers in the city of Baltimore. The firm of Jacob I. Cohen, Jr., and Brothers was known nationally for its honesty and integrity. Jacob I. Cohen, Jr., the leading partner, joined Solomon Etting in promoting passage of the Jew Bill. In 1826 Cohen was elected to the City Council, and he served as its president from 1845 on. He was also a founder of Baltimore's public school system, a commissioner of finance for the city, and the first president of the Philadelphia, Wilmington, & Baltimore Railroad. Benjamin I. Cohen, another of the brothers, was a socially prominent Baltimorean and an officer of the German Society of Maryland, probably the oldest benevolent organization in the state; he is reputed to have been a fine violinist and botanist. David I. Cohen, another member of

Jacob Hart, the patriotic merchant in eighteenth-century Baltimore who advanced money and supplies to General Lafayette during the Revolution. (*American Jewish Archives, Cincinnati*)

the dynasty, was an organizer of the Baltimore Stock Exchange. His brother Mendes I. Cohen fought in the War of 1812, served in the Maryland House of Delegates, and later became a world traveler; he was a benefactor of Johns Hopkins University.

In 1797 Solomon Etting, later joined by Jacob I. Cohen, Jr., offered the first of many petitions to the Maryland legislature requesting equal rights for Jews in Christian Maryland. They all were rejected by the legislature, but led by the Etting and Cohen families, the struggle went on. In 1818 Thomas Kennedy, a fine Christian and Jeffersonian, was elected to the legislature from Washington County. Year after year he championed the Jew Bill in the legislature but to no avail. In exasperation he wrote a friend, "Prejudice, prejudice is against the Bill, and you know prejudice has many followers." On the other hand, the editor of the *Maryland Censor* commented about the Jews: "They may and do fight our battles to the last drop of their

hearts' blood, yet they are shut out from the jury box, the bar and the bench! What bigotry!" Finally, in 1825, after Kennedy had gained the support of other prominent Christians, the bill was reluctantly passed by the legislature, more than twenty-five years after its introduction.

The first Jewish prayer meeting in Baltimore of which we have certain knowledge was held in the autumn of 1829 at the home of Zalma Rehine on Holiday Street. Rehine, born in Westphalia, spent most of his adult life as a merchant in Richmond but later moved to Baltimore. From that first meeting grew Congregation Nidche Israel, the Fugitives of Israel. Its house of worship, the Lloyd Street Synagogue, built in 1845, is the third oldest existing synagogue in the United States and has been designated a national historic place by the government. From the 1830s on, thousands of Jews settled in Baltimore, bringing with them a special concern for cultural and philanthropic activity.

FROM ITS INCEPTION the colony of Pennsylvania was liberal in its policy toward Jews. William Penn, the founder, was himself the victim of religious persecution. Expelled from Oxford for his Quakerism, Penn was imprisoned in the Tower of London for his religious writings and as a preacher who argued ably for freedom of conscience. Charles II, glad to see Penn quit England, granted him a charter for Pennsylvania, where religious and political freedom could flourish. In 1682 Penn and his Quaker followers arrived in the wilderness, gained the friendship of the Indians, and laid out a town to be called Philadelphia, the City of Brotherly Love. It was to become a world port and one of the largest cities in the United States.

Jewish fur traders from New York had set up Indian posts along the Pennsylvania side of the Delaware River years prior to the advent of William Penn, but little is known of them. Some of the earliest Jewish settlers in Pennsylvania were the Levys, Gratzes, Simons, Frankses, Phillipses, and Hayses.

Nathan Levy was born in London in 1704, a son of Moses Levy, the merchant prince of New York. Nathan Levy was to become a renowned Indian trader and shipowner. In 1737 he settled in Philadelphia and became the founder of Congregation Mikveh Israel, the Hope of Israel, in the 1740s, making it the third or fourth oldest Jewish congregation in America. He established the first Jewish cemetery in Philadelphia. His younger brother Samson Levy was a merchant who enjoyed a high social position among Philadelphians. He converted to Christianity to marry the well-born Martha Lampley. Moses Levy, their son, is credited as the first Jewish graduate of the College of Philadelphia (now the University of Pennsylvania), as well as America's first Jewish lawyer since he was admitted to the bar of Pennsylvania in 1778. Moses Levy held many public offices until 1822, when he was chosen chief judge of the district court of Philadelphia. He was also a trustee of the University of Pennsylvania. Judge Levy, a Jeffersonian, was several times attacked as a Jew by the antisemites of the Federalist party, leaving the good judge shocked and confused, for he considered himself an Episcopalian.

Levy Andrew Levy, unrelated to the Philadelphia Levys, settled prior to 1760 in the frontier town of Lancaster. From there he established a trading post at Fort Pitt (now Pittsburgh), and in partnership with Joseph Simon of Lancaster and the Gratzes of Philadelphia he took part in the development of

Reuben Etting of Baltimore, the revolutionary soldier who was appointed U.S. marshal for Maryland by President Thomas Jefferson. (*American Jewish Archives, Cincinnati*)

the Illinois Territory. Aaron Levy, born in Amsterdam, came to America in about 1760 and settled near Lancaster, much preferring frontier life to that of the city. He became wealthy as an Indian trader and land speculator and at times was associated with the redoubtable Joseph Simon, the Gratzes, and even Robert Morris, the rich Philadelphian who one day would become known as the Financier of the Revolution. During the Revolution Levy, a patriot, furnished supplies to the American troops and lent money to the Continental Congress.

In 1786 Aaron Levy founded the town of Aaronsburg in central Pennsylvania. He himself planned the site, and houses and streets were laid out with taste and skill. Levy donated two lots to the Salem Lutheran Church for the construction of a church, school, and cemetery. The consecration of the church marked one of the brightest moments in interfaith understanding in the United States. Aaronsburg, a monument to Levy, was the first of several American towns

Solomon Etting of Baltimore, younger brother of Reuben Etting, banker and proponent of the Jew Bill, was the first Jew to be elected to public office in Maryland. (*American Jewish Archives, Cincinnati*)

Jacob I. Cohen, Jr., the most prominent member of the prestigious Cohen clan of Maryland, was president of Baltimore's City Council and a founder of the city's public school system. (*American Jewish Archives, Cincinnati*)

named for a Jew. In 1796 Levy, no longer young, left the frontier for the more settled life of Philadelphia.

Joseph Simon, probably the first Jewish settler in the Lancaster area, began as a fur trader and at the height of his power was one of the biggest landowners in the colonies. Because of his efforts, a Jewish burial ground was set aside in frontier Lancaster as early as 1747. In partnership with the Gratz brothers, Levy Andrew Levy, Aaron Levy, and others, Simon was involved in land speculation as far west as Illinois. In the Revolution he furnished large quantities of rifles, ammunition, and other supplies to the American army.

The good Christian Thomas Kennedy, who championed the Jew Bill through the Maryland legislature in 1825. It provided equal rights for Jews in Christian Maryland. (*American Jewish Archives, Cincinnati*)

Downtown Philadelphia in 1754. Jews were established in the Quaker city long before then. (*The New York Public Library*)

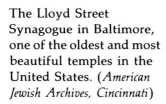

The Lloyd Street Synagogue in Baltimore, one of the oldest and most beautiful temples in the United States. (*American Jewish Archives, Cincinnati*)

An old view of Mikveh Israel in Philadelphia. In revolutionary times it was Haym Solomon's synagogue and a hotbed of patriotic zeal. (*American Jewish Archives, Cincinnati*)

Married twice, Simon fathered several daughters. His daughter Leah married Levy Phillips, the scion of a prominent Philadelphia family. Miriam was wedded to Michael Gratz, one of the Gratz brothers, in 1769. Rachel married the great Solomon Etting of Baltimore in 1783, and Susanna, the ambitious Levy Andrew Levy. Twenty-year-old Shinah Simon caused deep distress among Jews and Christians when she married Nicholas Schuyler, of the Philadelphia Schuylers. Joseph Simon died at ninety-one, the maker of many marriages and fortunes.

In Easton, Pennsylvania, an offshoot of Philadelphia, lived Myer Hart, a leading merchant and banker and one of the founders of the town in 1752. Another Jew in Easton was Michael Hart, apparently unrelated. Michael Hart, born in Germany, acquired considerable real estate in the burgeoning town. Although a pious Jew, he fought in the Revolutionary army. In 1780 he and Myer Hart headed the list of taxpayers in Easton.

One of the most prominent Jewish families in the colonies was the Gratzes of Philadelphia. Barnard Gratz, the founder, was born in Germany but lived in England for a time before settling in Philadelphia in 1754. His younger brother, Michael, after spending a year in India, joined him there. The Gratz brothers formed a lasting partnership in a trade house that became widely known in the colonies. Coastwise and West Indian shipping, land speculation in the West, banking, and the fur trade lay at the heart of their success. Their association with Joseph Simon, Michael Gratz's father-in-law, helped more than a little.

During the French and Indian War, the Gratz brothers supplied the British forces, but in the Revolution they were firm supporters of the American cause. It was Barnard who laid the cornerstone for the first synagogue in Philadelphia in 1782, while Michael fathered twelve children, several of whom became notable.

Benjamin Gratz, son of Michael, was graduated from the University of Pennsylvania in 1811 and served as an officer in the War of

Aaron Levy, American patriot and founder of the frontier town of Aaronsburg in central Pennsylvania in 1786. (*American Jewish Archives, Cincinnati*)

Judge Moses Levy of Philadelphia, grandson of the great Moses Levy of New York, suffered many antisemitic attacks, even as an Episcopalian. (*American Jewish Archives, Cincinnati*)

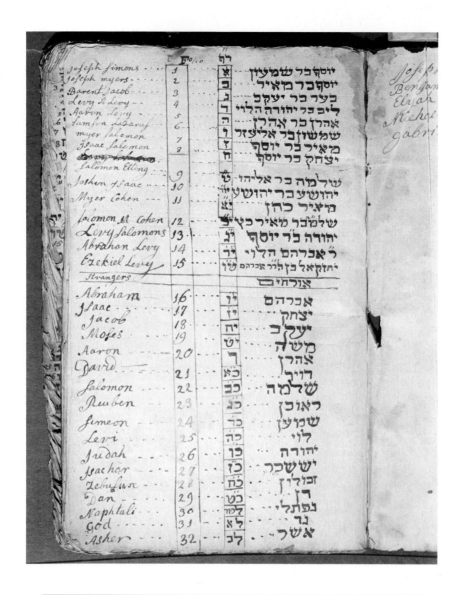

Page from the Synagogue Book of Lancaster, Pennsylvania; it is dated 1781. Joseph Simon or Simons, whose name heads the list, was a pioneer founder of Lancaster and one of the largest landholders in the colonies. (*American Jewish Archives, Cincinnati*)

1812. After the war he moved down to Kentucky, becoming one of the first Jewish settlers in that state. In Lexington he helped organize the Lexington & Ohio Railroad, became a member of the first City Council of Lexington, and was one of the founders of the Bank of Kentucky. Benjamin Gratz was a close friend of Kentucky's Henry Clay, and one of his daughters married into the Clay family.

Hyman Gratz, another of Michael Gratz's sons, remained in Philadelphia, where he became an active worker for the Federalist party, a director of the Pennsylvania Company for Life Insurance, one of the founders of the Pennsylvania Academy of Fine Arts, and a manager of the Jewish Publication Society, organized in Philadelphia in 1845. Jacob, a brother and business partner, was graduated from the University of Pennsylvania in 1807; four years later he received a Master of Arts degree. Jacob became president of the Union Canal Company and a perennial state legislator. Richea Gratz,

Barnard Gratz, the elder of the two Gratz brothers of Philadelphia, who became famous in the colonies for his vast financial enterprises. During the Revolution the brothers were staunch supporters of the patriot cause. (*American Jewish Archives, Cincinnati*)

Benjamin Gratz, the brother of Rebecca Gratz, left Philadelphia for Kentucky after the War of 1812. He became a close friend of Kentucky's Henry Clay. (*American Jewish Archives, Cincinnati*)

Michael Gratz, the younger of the Gratz brothers, was the father of twelve children, several of whom became notable, including the beautiful Rebecca. (*American Jewish Archives, Cincinnati*)

The Thomas Sully
portrait of the young
Rebecca Gratz of
Philadelphia. (*American
Jewish Archives, Cincinnati*)

one of Jacob's sisters, went to Marshall College in Lancaster. She was probably the first Jewish girl to go to college in the United States. However, it was to be her younger sister, Rebecca, who would become the outstanding American Jewess of her time and the most famous member of the family.

The beautiful Rebecca Gratz was born in Philadelphia in 1781. She attended finishing school along with the daughters of other rich Philadelphians, but all her life she continued to read, an activity that led to a cultivation of mind and spirit unusual for a woman of her time. The belle of Philadelphia society, she was much sought after by the fashionable, not only because of her beauty and wealth but also be-

cause of her keen and sympathetic mind. Her letters, of which there are many, reveal a noble spirit aware of politics, new books, the Bible, and the health and welfare of her family and friends. She had many gentile beaux, one of whom, Samuel Ewing, the handsome and literary son of Dr. John Ewing, provost of the University of Pennsylvania, she loved. But Rebecca would not marry outside her faith. In a letter to a friend she wrote: "My most cherished friends have generally been worshippers of a different faith than mine, and I have not loved them less on that account."

This idealistic figure of romance was friendly with many men of letters, including the great Washington Irving, who frequently enjoyed the hospitality of the Gratz home. When Irving visited Sir Walter Scott in Britain, he told the famous novelist about Rebecca, her beauty and kindness, her dedication to the poor and the sick, her loyalty to her religion. Scott, then pondering the story of Ivanhoe, was fascinated. Rebecca Gratz was to become the heroine of *Ivanhoe* as Rebecca, daughter of Isaac of York. When Scott sent a copy of his novel to Washington Irving, he wrote: "How do you like your Rebecca? Does the Rebecca I have pictured here compare well with the pattern given?"

Her portrait was painted by two famous American artists of the period, E. G. Malbone and Thomas Sully. Sully said of her, "Possessed of an elegant bearing, a melodiously sympathetic voice, a simple and frank and gracious womanliness, there was about Rebecca Gratz all that a princess of the blood Royal might have coveted."

Her charity and philanthropy showed themselves early. At twenty she became the tireless secretary of the first nonsectarian society organized to help the poor of Philadelphia. It was known as the Female Association for the Relief of Women and Children in Reduced Circumstance. A local newspaper commented on the organization that "All Philadelphia knows and appreciates their services." Rebecca

The mature and beautiful Rebecca Gratz in the early nineteenth century. (*American Jewish Archives, Cincinnati*)

Jonas Phillips, the
wealthy and influential
fur trader in colonial
Philadelphia. Both Uriah
Phillips Levy and
Mordecai Manuel Noah
were his grandsons.
(*American Jewish Archives,
Cincinnati*)

an apprenticeship with Haym Solomon and became a prominent merchant and broker. Isaac Hays, the son of Samuel and grandson of old Isaac, had a distinguished career in medicine. He received his M.D. degree from the University of Pennsylvania in 1820 and within a few years was recognized as an outstanding practitioner and one of America's foremost ophthalmologists. He wrote extensively in the medical sciences and became editor of the *American Journal of the Medical Sciences* in Philadelphia. Dr. Hays was a founder of the American Medical Association and the author of its code of ethics, which attempted to place the American medical profession on the highest possible plane.

Jonas Phillips, one of the progenitors of the Phillips family of New York and Philadelphia, was born in Germany in 1736. He spent time in Charleston and in New York but finally settled in Philadelphia, where he enjoyed success as a fur merchant. He was also a soldier in the Philadelphia militia. Naphtali, his son, removed to New York, where he became publisher of the *National Advocate* and for more than seventy years was a prominent member of

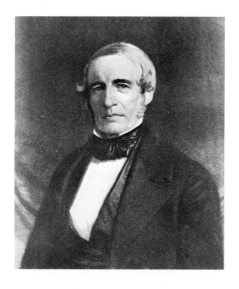

Dr. Isaac Hays of Philadelphia, one of America's foremost physicians and a founder of the American Medical Association. (*American Jewish Archives, Cincinnati*)

was also founder and secretary for forty years of the Philadelphia Orphan Asylum. In 1819 she helped organize the Female Hebrew Benevolent Society for the benefit of "indigent sisters of the House of Israel." It was the first American Jewish women's group. This grand lady drew up plans for the first Hebrew Sunday school in America and was its president for twenty-six years. Rebecca Gratz died at eighty-eight, a spinster mourned by all.

Isaac Hays came to America from Holland in 1720. His son Samuel was born in New York but settled in Philadelphia, where he served

1760. Her grandfather was the wealthy Jacob Franks of New York, and her father, the well-known David Franks of Philadelphia, purveyor of military supplies to Colonel George Washington during the French and Indian War. David, who married Margaret Evans in 1743, permitted his wife to rear their children as Anglicans. The Frankses, as it happened, were one of the few American Jewish families to support the British in the Revolution.

Young Rebecca reigned as an acknowledged belle, renowned for grace and wit, in Philadelphia society. Revolutionary Philadelphia was the national capital from 1777 to 1788

Lady Rebecca Johnson, the social lioness of Bath, England. She was born Rebecca Franks in Philadelphia, the daughter of the controversial David Franks. (*American Jewish Historical Society, Waltham, Mass.*)

An eighteenth-century portrait of Abigail Franks, the sister of Rebecca Franks and the wife of a Philadelphia Hamilton. (*American Jewish Archives, Cincinnati*)

Tammany Hall. Another son, Zalegman, was graduated from the University of Pennsylvania in 1795; an attorney and a politician, he was an ardent Jacksonian Democrat. Aaron, his brother, was a playwright, actor, and theater operator, while Manuel was a physician who fought in the War of 1812 and died mysteriously in Veracruz, Mexico. Another Phillips of Philadelphia was Israel Phillips, who in 1772 was jailed for receiving stolen goods but escaped, to what end no one knows.

The fashionable Lady Rebecca Johnson was born Rebecca Franks of Philadelphia in and the seat of the Continental Congress. It was not only the political heart of the country but its leading social center with a brilliant and often frivolous life in which, despite the war, patriots and Tories continued to vie in friendly rivalry for social supremacy. In 1777 General William Howe temporarily captured the city and established his headquarters there. The American government was compelled to seek refuge at York, Pennsylvania, and General George Washington was driven to spend the heartbreaking winter in Valley Forge, while the handsome and aristocratic young English officers attached to General Howe's army added a lively and colorful element to the social life of the ladies of Philadelphia.

An ardent Tory and socialite, Rebecca Franks was chosen one of the two "Queens of Beauty" when the British staged a gorgeous fete in honor of Sir Henry Clinton, the new commander of the British army in America. A great pageant and grand regatta, followed by a series of tableaux and a procession through triumphal arches, and ending with a grand ball, marked the entertainment. Though thrilling to the Tories of Philadelphia, the celebration proved premature. Within a few months the American army recaptured Philadelphia.

Patriot pressure in 1780 forced the David Franks family from Philadelphia to British-controlled New York, where they took up residence at old Jacob Franks's summer home in Flatbush, Brooklyn. At twenty-two Rebecca married, in New York, Lieutenant Colonel Henry Johnson, an officer in the British army. It was a social event reported in the *New York Gazette and Weekly Mercury* of January 1782. Soon after, the happily married couple moved to England to make their home in Bath, the very fashionable spa of eighteenth- and nineteenth-century England. By 1809, when Johnson retired from the army, he had become a general, and nine years later he was created a baronet. In the years that passed, Rebecca Franks, now Lady Rebecca Johnson, the matron of Bath, quite naturally assumed leadership in the social life of the resort.

In 1816 Winfield Scott, then an American general of twenty-nine, fresh from his triumphs in the War of 1812, visited the stately Lady Rebecca at Bath. He recalled that when he was a boy, the former Rebecca Franks was still celebrated for her brilliance, beauty, and wit. He reported that on their first meeting she exclaimed, "I have gloried in my rebel countrymen!" Then pointing to heaven, with both hands, she added, "Would to God I, too, had been a patriot." The rich, well-married socialite died at sixty-three.

Philadelphia Jewry provided history with several Revolutionary War heroes. Solomon Bush, the son of Mathias Bush, a prominent merchant and shipowner, served as deputy adjutant general of the Pennsylvania militia. He was severely wounded in action, and when the British took Philadelphia in 1777, he was imprisoned. After the war he was retired with the rank of lieutenant colonel. George and Lewis Bush, both majors in the Revolutionary army, may have been Solomon Bush's cousins. Lewis Bush died of wounds inflicted at the Battle of Brandywine.

Benjamin Franks was a jeweler in New York in 1696. Poor and bored, he joined Captain William Kidd, the legendary pirate, to seek his fortune. Unfortunately his dreams were never realized, and Franks vanished in India, after a Captain Kidd raid on the subcontinent. His son Moses Benjamin Franks was a Jewish tailor in New York and Philadelphia and the father of Isaac Franks, the Revolutionary hero. Isaac Franks settled in Philadelphia, was successfully engaged in land speculation, and in 1776 enlisted in the American forces. During the war he served in many capacities, including quartermaster or foragemaster. He was captured by the British but escaped. A brave soldier, Franks was placed on General Washington's staff, and in 1793 he was host to then President Washington at his home in Germantown when the president left Philadelphia to escape a yellow fever epidemic. A year later Franks was appointed lieutenant colonel of a Philadelphia regiment. Gilbert Stuart painted Isaac Franks's portrait. It is doubtful that these Frankses were related to the rich Frankses of New York and Philadelphia.

David Salisbury Franks was born in Philadelphia but moved to Canada, where his father, Abraham, gained prominence as a Quebec mer-

Colonel Isaac Franks of New York
and Philadelphia, a hero of the
Revolutionary War. (*American Jewish
Historical Society, Waltham, Mass.*)

A rare portrait of Major Benjamin Nones, the Revolutionary War hero who rescued the fatally wounded Baron de Kalb from the bloody field of battle. Nones, a Sephardic Jew, was several times cited for conspicuous gallantry. (*American Jewish Archives, Cincinnati*)

Colonel David Salisbury Franks, aide-de-camp to General Benedict Arnold, was accused and then fully exonerated of all charges of complicity in Arnold's treachery. (*American Jewish Archives, Cincinnati*)

chant. Young Franks, himself a merchant and an ardent rebel, provided funds and supplies to the American army in Canada, an act of treason against George III. When the Americans were driven from Canada in 1776, Franks prudently fled south to Massachusetts, where he immediately enlisted in the Revolutionary forces.

He rose rapidly through the ranks and in 1778 was appointed aide-de-camp to General Benedict Arnold, a fateful promotion for David Salisbury Franks. When Arnold turned traitor to the American cause, fingers were pointed at his trusted Jewish aide, Franks. Near disgrace, the patriot soldier stood trial for his general's treason and was promptly acquitted. Not satisfied with the terms of the acquittal, Franks applied to General Washington for a special court of inquiry, which completely exonerated him. He was promoted to the rank of lieutenant colonel and after the war went on several diplomatic missions for his country. For Franks's ser-

Valley Forge in the desperate winter of 1777–1778. Jewish patriots suffered with their gentile comrades-in-arms. (*American Jewish Archives, Cincinnati*)

vices, the American government awarded him a large grant of land. Franks once wrote: "I devoted . . . the best part of my life to the Service of my Country, in all which time, I am bold to say that I have ever been actuated by a disinterested Zeal for her Honor and Prosperity."

The German Baron Johann de Kalb, who died in action, commanded a regiment of Revolutionary soldiers, so many of whom were Jews that it was often called the Jewish regiment. Among his officers was Major Benjamin Nones, a wine dealer from Bordeaux, courageous and picturesque, who was drawn to America to fight for freedom. He arrived in Philadelphia in 1777, along with the Marquis de Lafayette, and promptly joined the Revolutionary army. A private at twenty, he soon rose to the rank of major for conspicuous gallantry in action, especially during the Battle of Savannah. Nones was one of a few combat troopers who went through the entire Revolutionary War. At Camden, South Carolina, in 1780 it was he and two other Jewish officers, Captain Jacob De Leon and Captain Jacob De la Motta, who carried the mortally wounded Baron de Kalb from the bloody field of battle. General Casimir Pulaski once cited Nones for valor because "his behavior under fire in all the bloody actions we fought have been marked by the bravery and courage which a military man is expected to show for the liberties of his country."

After the war the veteran soldier returned to Philadelphia, where he entered into partnership with Haym Solomon. But his vision of wealth vanished with the untimely death of Solomon in 1785. Broke and barely able to feed his growing family, Major Nones was granted an appointment as a Spanish and French interpreter to the American government. He ran for public office as a steadfast and vocal supporter of Thomas Jefferson but was defeated by the Federalists who assailed the Revolutionary hero as a Jew. "I am a Jew," the militant Nones replied, "I glory in belonging to that persuasion.

I am poor; I am so, my family is also large, but soberly and decently brought up. They have not been taught to revile a Christian because his religion is not so old as theirs. They have not been taught to mock at conscientious belief."

Several Jewish soldiers, including Dr. Philip Moses Russell, Washington's surgeon, suffered the hardships of Valley Forge. He was kept busy during that terrible winter. Not all American Jews were officers in the army of the Revolution; most were ordinary riflemen. Asher Pollock from Newport enlisted in 1777 for the duration. According to regimental records, he was then fifty-two years old, born in London, and five feet five inches in height. This inconspicuous private served the patriot cause for

Robert Morris, a signer of the Declaration of Independence, often referred to his colleague Haym Solomon as "our little friend on Front Street." (*The New York Public Library*)

Haym Solomon of Philadelphia, the Polish Jew who became a
great American patriot. His reputation for honesty and integrity
in international financial circles lent credibility to the
revolutionary cause. (*American Jewish Archives, Cincinnati*)

more than six long years and was awarded two
badges of honor. Asher was the typical winter
soldier of Valley Forge, unsung and uncele-
brated. Another rifleman was Cusham Polack
of Georgia, who fared better than Asher. When
Polack was discharged, he received a formal
certificate from the Georgia delegation to the
Continental Congress stating that this Jewish
private, "a citizen of the state of Georgia for
many years past, gave early demonstration of
his attachment to the American cause, by tak-
ing an active part, in several engagements

against the enemy, when he behaved with ap-
probation."

Robert Morris, the most prominent merchant in America in Revolutionary times, became the so-called Financier of the American
Revolution, as we have noted. Financing the
war was, if possible, an even more formidable
task than soldiering. Morris, a gifted Philadelphia businessman, knew or was in partnership
with many Jewish merchants and speculators
in the colonies. Energetic and decisive, the gentile Morris called on his Jewish friends for funds

The Isaacs House in East Hampton, Long Island, as it looked in the mid-nineteenth century. Aaron Isaacs, the Jewish founder of the family, settled in the wilderness of the Hamptons in colonial times. His grandson John Howard Payne was the author of "Home Sweet Home." (*American Jewish Archives, Cincinnati*)

whenever the Revolution was reeling toward bankruptcy, as was often the case. The Levys and the Seixas family of New York, the Gratzes of Philadelphia, the Minis and Sheftall families of Savannah were among his many contributors, but the halo of history came to rest on the head of Morris's friend, the great Haym Solomon of Philadelphia.

A man of brilliant financial mind, Haym Solomon was born in Leszno, Poland. While still young, he traveled widely in Europe and in England, working in financial houses, learning the complexities of international finance, and establishing important banking connections. From the day he landed in New York in the 1770s he was a patriot. When the war broke out, Solomon, then in his early thirties, undertook to supply American troops in British-dominated New York. Captured by the British, the Polish immigrant was imprisoned in several different and dismal jails. When General Heister of the Hessians discovered that Sol-

omon spoke many languages, he had the Jew released from prison and appointed him staff interpreter and sutler to the Hessian troops. While carrying out his duties, Solomon secretly aided in the escape of many American prisoners of war and even persuaded some Hessian officers and troops to desert and join the patriot cause. His activities were uncovered by the British, and Solomon, now under a death sentence, fled to American-held Philadelphia. He and his wife, Rachel, the sister of the Revolutionary soldier Isaac Franks, bought a house on Front Street from which the financier conducted his business.

Solomon was a great success in Philadelphia because most of the commerce of the port was with foreign markets the trade conditions of which he knew intimately. His reputation for honesty and integrity gained him an appointment as agent for the French government and paymaster for the French forces in America, which supported the Americans in their struggle for freedom. So adept was he in financial transactions that he quickly came to the notice of Robert Morris, then superintendent of finance to the Revolutionary government. Solomon, the patriot financier, was designated broker to the infant Republic. At the beginning of Morris's diary he referred to Solomon as his "Jew broker," but as the months wore on and financial problems were reaching the insurmountable, Morris noted, almost on a daily basis, "I sent for Haym Solomon today" or "I spoke to my little friend on Front Street."

Solomon handled hundreds of bills of exchange for the new government, negotiated domestic and foreign loans, endorsed notes, subscribed to all government bonds, and from his own pocket equipped American troops and gave generously to needy soldiers and statesmen, among whom were Thomas Jefferson, James Madison, and James Monroe, three future presidents of the United States. When he

died at forty-five, from a lingering illness contracted in a British jail, Haym Solomon was insolvent. His wealth had been invested in government loans, which Congress refused to honor. Rachel and her four young children left Philadelphia and were taken in by relatives in New York. For years the son of the Revolutionary financier, Haym M. Solomon, fought to recover his father's money from the government, with no success. If one thinks this a shabby example of antisemitism, consider the case of Robert Morris himself: When he went bankrupt in 1798, the American government stood by, with evenhanded indifference, as Morris, a signer of the Declaration of Independence, was sentenced to three years in debtors' prison. Solomon, the adopted American patriot, is also known in history books as Salomon.

In 1788 Congregation Mikveh Israel of Philadelphia found itself in difficult financial straits. Haym Solomon, one of the two or three major contributors to the synagogue, was dead, and the Jewish patriots of New York, who for a time swelled the ranks of the worshipers, had returned to their own congregation, Shearith Israel. An appeal by the congregation was made to Philadelphians, "worthy fellow citizens of every Religious Denomination," to come to their aid, and they did. Benjamin Franklin, David Rittenhouse of the Philadelphia Rittenhouses, and William Bradford, the printer, were listed among the subscribers.

THE REVOLUTIONARY WAR became serious in August 1776, when the British attacked Long Island in force. Jews had settled on the island prior to the 1750s. In East Hampton was Aaron Isaacs and his brood, while other Jewish families were found in Islip and Jamaica. Washington's small army was defeated at Brooklyn Heights, and the British were in control of New York and Long Island Sound. After several years of marching, countermarching, misery, and anguish, the British accepted defeat at Yorktown, Virginia, in 1781, where Lord Cornwallis surrendered to the American and French forces under General Washington.

When Washington became president, the honorable old soldier wrote to the Jewish con-

General George Washington, the most honorable of soldiers, personally thanked the colonial Jews of America for their loyalty and support during the Revolution. (*The New York Public Library*)

gregations of New York, Newport, Philadelphia, Savannah, Richmond, and Charleston. In the stately style of the eighteenth century, Washington wisely observed to Newport: "It is now no more that toleration is spoken of, as if it were by the indulgence of one class of people, that another enjoyed the exercise of their inherent natural rights. For happily the Government of the United States, which gives to bigotry no sanction, to persecution no assistance, requires only that they who live under its protection should demean themselves as good citizens. . . ." And further: "May the children of the Stock of Abraham, who dwell in this land . . . sit in safety under his own vine and figtree and there shall be none to make him afraid." The latter is a quote from the Hebrew prophet Micah.

Thomas Jefferson, one of the finest minds this country has ever produced, made religious freedom a cardinal American principle. It was the great Virginian who wrote the Declaration of Independence, insisted on the Bill of Rights, fought for the separation of church and state, and, even after the Constitution had been accepted, was concerned enough about intolerance to write: "But more remains to be done. For altho' we are free by the law, we are not so in practice. Public opinion erects itself into an Inquisition, and exercises its office with as much fanaticism as fans the flames of an Auto da fe."

Overwhelmingly the American Jews supported Jefferson even if the witty Virginian thought that the "Stock of Abraham" took itself too seriously; after all, he was a Southern gentleman of humor and imagination, much more than anyone could say about that crowd in New England. In the years to come the assimilated Jew tended toward the Federalist party, the conservative, law-and-order party, but the Jeffersonian Jew, the unreconstructed Jew, remained loyal to the Democratic party of Jefferson.

In his monumental work *History of the Rise and Influence of the Spirit of Rationalism in Europe,* published in 1865, William E. H. Lecky, the distinguished British historian, commented that "the Hebraic mortar cemented the foundations of American democracy." Not only did American Jews give of themselves and of their blood and treasure in the hard days of the Revolution, but their Holy Scriptures, the Old Testament, provided an arsenal of rhetoric from which the apostles of rebellion drew inspiration for their attack on king and country. From pulpits throughout the land resounded the story of the Exodus, when the Children of Israel shook off their Egyptian oppressors. King Rehoboam's insolence, which drove the tribes of Israel to defiance, was an oft-repeated tale. The ancient Hebrew prophets, the denouncers of kings, were fully appreciated by defenders of the patriot cause. Even the inscription on the Liberty Bell itself—"Proclaim liberty throughout all the land unto all the inhabitants thereof"—was drawn from Leviticus. The foundations of the new American democracy had been laid, and the Jews, that most ancient of peoples, had played a historic role.

Drawn from the Old Testament Leviticus is the inscription on the Liberty Bell: "Proclaim liberty throughout all the land unto all the inhabitants thereof." (*The New York Public Library*)

PART FOUR

◀ A rare photograph of Sergeant David Urbansky of Ohio relaxing before battle. His coolness and bravery under heavy Confederate fire at Shiloh and again at Vicksburg won him the Congressional Medal of Honor. (*American Jewish Archives, Cincinnati*)

Westward Ho and
the Civil War

WHILE THE NATION was engaged in a crucial Revolution, American pioneers and frontiersmen, both Jew and gentile, were pressing ever west. From the Atlantic seaboard to the grasslands of the Middle West to the new territories of the Southeast the flow of sturdy migrants followed the courses of great rivers and toiled over mountain trails, conquering prairie and forest, warring against hostile Indians, and winning a new independence, a new freedom from the confining spirit of city life and its issue, civilization.

Some of the earliest Jewish frontiersmen in Middle America have already been mentioned, but Jacob Franks, John Hays, and Chapman Abrahams are worthy of note. Franks, one of Wisconsin's pioneers, was in 1792 in Green Bay, where he established several mills that helped develop the region. John Hays arrived in Cahokia, the first permanent settlement in Illinois, in 1793. A fur trader, he later became first postmaster, then sheriff and in 1813 was appointed tax collector for the territory. In 1762 Chapman Abrahams became the first Jewish settler in Detroit, a fort-village in the wilderness. During the Indian rebellion he was captured by Pontiac but released. Another frontier trader in the Michigan Territory was Ezekiel Solomon. He, too, was captured during the Pontiac uprising in 1763. Adam Gimbel, of a later period, was a storekeeper in Vincennes, Indiana, prior to 1840. His policies in merchandising—return and refund, the one-price store, the variety of goods under a single roof—were unheard-of innovations. They were to make him the founder of a department store dynasty.

In the great Southeast, in the territories of Mississippi and Alabama, was the Monsanto family of Natchez, the rich river port now famous for its antebellum mansions. Plantation owners, the Monsantos were in Mississippi before 1783, while Chapman Levy, a hero of the War of 1812, was a planter near Camden, Mississippi. Abraham Mordecai, sometimes called the founder of Montgomery, Alabama, arrived there in 1785. It is said that he lived for fifty years in the Creek Nation, took an Indian as his wife, and studied Indian customs. In 1804 Mordecai built the first cotton gin in Montgomery.

President Jefferson and Napoleon of France concluded the Louisiana Purchase in 1803. A vast land area, the Louisiana Territory more than doubled the size of the United States. In whole or in part fourteen states were to be carved from the territory, stretching from Louisiana in the South through the Great Plains to Montana, Wyoming, and Colorado in the Northwest. For about $15 million Jefferson and his envoys had closed one of the great land deals in history. Napoleon felt that the territory could not be defended by the French, and besides, he needed money for his military ventures in Europe. Americans were largely bored with the acquisition of wilderness but eyed the port of New Orleans with joy.

A year before the purchase Judah Touro settled in New Orleans. The son of Rabbi Touro of Newport and the nephew of Moses Michael Hays, who had brought him up, young Judah was twenty-seven at the time. An orphan at twelve, and later a lonely bachelor, brilliant in business, Touro became one of the richest men in New Orleans and an early American philanthropist without parallel. Within a few years Judah Touro had established himself as a prom-

John Hays, Jewish pioneer and frontiersman, arrived in Cahokia, the first permanent settlement in Illinois, in 1793. (*American Jewish Archives, Cincinnati*)

Gravestone of Abraham Mordecai, the reputed founder of Montgomery, Alabama. (*American Jewish Archives, Cincinnati*)

inent merchant shipper in the port and was widely respected by his fellow French and Spanish settlers for his business acumen and his honesty and integrity. His mercantile pursuits prospered greatly, and Touro, the young American Jew from Newport and Boston, entered real estate. In later years he was a real estate magnate and the leading shipowner in New Orleans, the queen city of the Mississippi.

During the War of 1812 he enlisted in the army of Andrew Jackson to defend his adopted city against a British onslaught. At the ensuing Battle of New Orleans Judah Touro, on a hazardous mission, was severely wounded and left to die. A comrade-in-arms, Rezin Davis Shepherd, a true Christian, carried Touro to a field hospital where surgeons saved his life. For more than forty years after that act of devotion Touro and Shepherd were inseparable companions. Touro spoke of him as "my dear, old and devoted friend, to whom, under Divine Providence, I am greatly indebted for the preservation of my life."

One of the few Jews in New Orleans at the time, Touro nonetheless followed his faith. He was well known for closing his business on Saturday and was described as "A plainly dressed old man, sitting in the corner, devoutly engaged in prayer." Though wealthy, he lived in a small apartment and daily opened and closed his business himself.

"A noble Israelite snatched us from the jaws of destruction," wrote the minister of the First Congregational Church of New Orleans after Judah Touro had given him the funds to build a new church, the old one having burned down. Touro's philanthropy is legendary. He

Judah Touro of New Orleans, one of America's most renowned philanthropists. An Orthodox Jew, he refused to remove his hat for the portrait. (*American Jewish Archives, Cincinnati*)

Joseph Jonas, Jewish pioneer in the Ohio Territory. He settled in Cincinnati in 1817. (*American Jewish Archives, Cincinnati*)

built a free public library in New Orleans, the first of its kind in the United States, founded the Touro Infirmary, one of the South's best hospitals, and erected an almshouse and several orphanages. He also built a synagogue.

When, in 1840, it seemed that, for lack of funds, the building of the Bunker Hill Monument would have to be abandoned, Touro came forward with a donation of $10,000 to prevent the failure of the enterprise. He and his brother, Abraham, saved the historic synagogue in Newport where their father had worshiped and left money for other good causes in the Rhode Island city. In his remarkable will Judah Touro gave substantial gifts to more than

Rezin Davis Shepherd, the Christian soldier who saved Judah Touro's life at the Battle of New Orleans. In subsequent years Touro made him a rich man. (*American Jewish Archives, Cincinnati*)

sixty organizations and individuals, Jewish and Christian alike. This unparalleled example of charity knew limitations of neither creed nor geography: $80,000 to New Orleans for an almshouse; $20,000 to New York's Jews' Hospital, later renamed Mount Sinai; $10,000 to Massachusetts General Hospital; and $60,000 to "our unfortunate Jewish brethren in Jerusalem and the Holy Land." These were unheard-of sums for the time.

At seventy-eight this simple, brave, and revered Jew died. He was buried at Newport, where his tombstone bears the epitaph "The last of his name, he inscribed it in the book of philanthropy, to be remembered forever."

MANY AMERICAN JEWS served in the War of 1812, often called our Second War of Independence. For almost three years the war was fiercely fought on land and sea, and even the White House was burned by the vindictive British. Uriah Phillips Levy, a naval commander during that war, was a patriot and fighting Jew. The son of Michael Levy, a soldier in the Revolutionary army, Uriah was born in Philadelphia in 1792. At the tender age of ten he shipped out to sea as a cabin boy, and by twenty he was captain of the schooner *George Washington*. A year later his crew mutinied and left young Levy stranded on an island. Never one to avoid a fight, Levy worked his way back home, charged the mutineers, and brought them to justice.

When the War of 1812 broke out, Levy immediately enlisted and was commissioned as sailing master in the United States Navy. First on the *Alert* and then on the brig *Argus*, Levy captured several prizes until he himself was captured; he spent the remainder of the war in a British prison. At sea, it is said, Levy spent Saturday in his quarters unless a battle was pressing. Only in an emergency would he break the Sabbath. After the war Levy served on many missions, including the suppression of piracy and the elimination of the slave trade in Honduras Bay, and as commander of the U.S. Mediterranean fleet.

However, the sea warrior is most memorable as the center of controversy. Levy suffered several career setbacks in the navy because of antisemitism and the natural snobbishness of naval officers who had not risen from the ranks as he had. The fiery-tempered Levy was court-martialed six times and twice dismissed from the navy for insubordination and dueling. In one duel he killed a fellow officer for antisemitic slurs. Several times reduced in rank, Levy demanded vindication, and in 1855 Congress ordered a special court of inquiry, which fully cleared him of all charges and restored him to rank. In his own defense, he wrote: "At an early day, and especially from the time it became known to the officers of my age and grade that I aspired to a lieutenancy, I was forced to encounter a large share of the prejudices and hostility by which, for so many ages, the Jew has been pursued. I ask you to unite with the wisest and best men of our own country and of Europe in denouncing these sentiments, not only as injurious to the peace and welfare of the community, but as repugnant to every dictate of

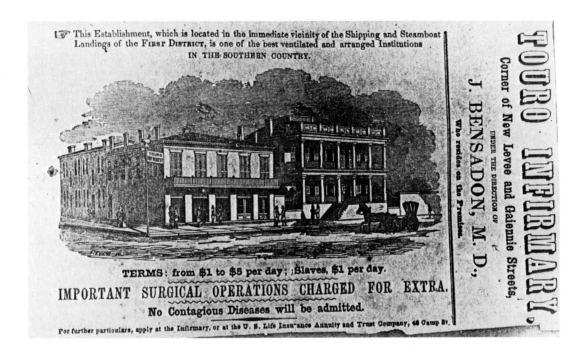

Advertisement for the Touro Infirmary before the Civil War. It was founded by Judah Touro of New Orleans. (*American Jewish Archives, Cincinnati*)

reason, humanity and justice." Before he retired, Levy was promoted to commodore, the highest rank in the United States Navy at the time.

In later life the spirited Levy became wealthy, and with part of his fortune he bought and renovated the beautiful home of his favorite hero, Thomas Jefferson, at Monticello, Virginia. Levy asked the government to make it a national shrine. He also donated a statue of the great democrat to Congress.

While in the navy, Levy became violently opposed to having seamen flogged for breaking rules and banned the common practice on ships under his command. That created another storm of controversy. Levy pressed forward, as always, and Congress finally passed a law abolishing corporal punishment in the United States Navy. Levy, the fearless Jew, wished to

be remembered not for his long and distinguished service to his country but simply as "the father of the law for the abolition of the barbarous practice of corporal punishment in the Navy of the United States." Dead at seventy, Commodore Levy was buried in Long Island, New York.

DIFFERENT FROM Uriah Phillips Levy was Mordecai Manuel Noah, a quixotic intellectual who became the most talked-about Jew of his time. Noah was born in Philadelphia in 1785, the son of a Revolutionary soldier and Zipporah Phillips, the daughter of the rich Jonas Phillips of Philadelphia; she died when Mordecai was only seven. Mordecai Noah was first cousin to the sailor Uriah Phillips Levy, and while Levy never walked away from a fight, Noah never

98

Uriah Phillips Levy, the
young and handsome
naval lieutenant.
(*American Jewish Archives,
Cincinnati*)

The synagogue built by Judah Touro in New Orleans.
(*American Jewish Archives, Cincinnati*)

The great New England sailing vessel *Judah Touro* was named in
honor of the famous philanthropist. (*American Jewish Archives,
Cincinnati*)

Commodore Uriah Phillips Levy, the mature and courageous
American sailor. (*American Jewish Archives, Cincinnati*)

shied away from publicity. During his tenure as sheriff of New York, Mordecai Manuel Noah was attacked by an outraged citizen, who complained, saying, "Fine thing, that a Jew should be hanging Christians!" Sheriff Noah replied, "Fine Christians, to need hanging by anyone!"

Self-educated, flamboyant, and ambitious, Noah made for himself careers as journalist and playwright, diplomat, politician, and judge. In the rough-and-tumble days between the War of 1812 and the Mexican War, such versatility was not uncommon. A newspaper reporter in Philadelphia, he became editor of a journal in Charleston that promoted the War of 1812 and supported the aspirations of James Madison. At twenty-four Noah was a war hawk and a duelist who had gained many enemies. Soon after hostilities began between Britain and the United States, President Madison appointed Noah consul to Tunis on the Barbary Coast, where he obtained the release of Americans held hostage by Barbary pirates. His enemies in Washington conspired to have him removed and were successful when the secretary of state affirmed that Noah's religion disqualified him for the post.

Mordecai Noah, less than defeated, returned to his country and established himself in New York, where he became prominent as politician, newspaper publisher, and dramatist. His flair for the theatrical and his eloquence cast an aura around the remainder of his career. Angered at his dismissal, he set himself up as spokesman of his people. "I find my own government insulting the religious feelings of a whole nation," he wrote. He was sheriff of New York, surveyor of the port, and editor or founder of several newspapers, including the *New York Enquirer,* the *Evening Star,* and the *National Advocate.* Many of his plays were produced in New York theaters, and in later life he was appointed judge on the New York court of sessions.

But his abiding interest was in the history and plight of the Jewish people. Albeit a talented man of practical affairs, in his own mind Noah conceived of himself as the divinely elected leader of the Jews, a great genius, and the judge of a restored Israel. After several fan-

Mordecai Manuel Noah of New York, the most talked-about Jew of his time. (*American Jewish Archives, Cincinnati*)

tasy attempts to wrest, or buy, Palestine from the Turks, Noah struck on the idea of having a Jewish homeland in the United States, under the protection of the Constitution. The settlement, to be on Grand Island in the Niagara River, was to be called Ararat, after Mount Ararat of the Bible where Noah's Ark came to rest after the Great Flood. Mordecai Noah and his friends acquired a 17,000-acre tract on the small and uninhabited island near Buffalo, New York, and grandiloquently announced to the Jews of the world that their "City of Refuge," their asylum of freedom, was here, on the Niagara River. Noah, the protector of Israel, made headlines, especially in his own newspapers. He called for all the Jews of the earth to assemble on the Niagara frontier on September 15, 1825, for the great ingathering. Ararat, he said, was to be a temporary homeland until the Jews returned to the Holy Land, so long promised and foretold.

Noah, then forty, spent months planning elaborate ceremonies for the momentous day, the most dramatic event of his career. He even invited the Indian chiefs of the territory to participate since they were the descendants of the ten lost tribes. When the eventful day arrived, Mordecai Noah, the judge of Israel, was bedecked in regal splendor, in crimson silk robes trimmed with ermine. Ceremonies were held in the Episcopal Church of St. Paul in the frontier town of Buffalo, since the Reverend Searle was Noah's friend. Hundreds of onlookers applauded the imposing Noah as he led a colorful procession of military bands, state officials, clergymen, Masons in full regalia, and Indians into the church. A twenty-one-gun salute was offered. Inside the church the soaring music of Handel's *Judas Maccabeus* greeted the crowd as they viewed a large cornerstone laid on the communion table, which read: "Hear O Israel, the Lord is our God, the Lord is One. Ararat, a City of Refuge for the Jews, Founded by Mordecai Manuel Noah, in the month Tizri, 5586, Sept. 1825 & in the 50th year of American Independence." Noah, the cynosure of all eyes, delivered a rambling, pompous address to the assembly about Jews, Indians, patriotism, history, the theater, and the future of the world. The master showman seemed not to notice that there were no Jews present at the founding of Ararat. The City of Refuge, the Jewish homeland, was stillborn.

In later years Noah was denounced as a charlatan, a real estate speculator, and a Jew of overwhelming conceit. He was also celebrated as the world's first Zionist. Absurd and often ridiculous, Noah was America's first self-made Jewish celebrity. All that remains of Ararat is a weather-beaten cornerstone that rests in a glass case in the Buffalo Historical Museum.

BEFORE WE RETURN to the West, a word about Westchester, then a sparsely inhabited region north of New York City. Jewish fur traders had been dealing with the Indians there

Jacob Hays stalking criminals in early New York. Hays was New York City's chief of police for forty-five years, a record unequaled in the annals of American law enforcement. (*American Jewish Archives, Cincinnati*)

An engraving of the historic Alamo. Jewish frontiersmen fought and died for Texas independence. (*The New York Public Library*)

Jacob De Cordova, an American Jew of Sephardic origin, was a Texas pioneer long before Texas became a state. (*American Jewish Archives, Cincinnati*)

Henry Castro of Texas, who preferred to call himself Henri, comte de Castro, was a Jew of shady French origins who became Sam Houston's friend and a colonizer of Texas. (*American Jewish Archives, Cincinnati*)

since the late seventeenth century. Among its earliest settlers was the Hays family of German Jewish descent, who were in New York prior to the 1720s. Merchants and farmers, they pioneered such towns as Rye, Bedford, Pleasantville, and New Rochelle. Jacob Hays, the foremost of the Westchester Hayses, was born in Bedford in 1772. He moved to New York City when he was twenty-six and was appointed city marshal. So competent and courageous was Hays that in 1802 he was promoted to chief of police, a position he held for more than forty-five years. He enjoyed an international reputation as a law enforcer and detective.

TEXAS, EXPLORED BY the Spanish in the sixteenth century, became part of Mexico in the eighteenth century. Missions protected by presidios were established at San Antonio, Goliad, Nacogdoches, Laredo, and elsewhere, while hostile Indians, including the Apache and Comanche, roamed the territory. After the Louisiana Purchase had given the United States a common border with Texas, Americans looked at the Mexican province with covetous eyes and a keen sense of manifest destiny.

American adventurers from 1812 on attempted to disrupt Mexican rule, but with no success. In the early 1820s Moses and Stephen

Adolphus Sterne, Jewish pioneer in Texas in 1826 and a founder of the Republic of Texas. (*American Jewish Archives, Cincinnati*)

thousand Mexican troops laid siege to the small mission, and its garrison of fewer than 200 Texans and frontiersmen fell after a heroic stand. Among the dead were a few Jews, one of whom, Abraham Wolf, has been identified. A month later, after their surrender near Goliad, some 300 Texans were shot in cold blood by the Mexicans; several Jewish rebels were listed among the Texas dead. At the Battle of San Jacinto, soon after the Goliad massacre, Sam Houston and his gallant troop of Texans surprised and defeated a larger force of Mexicans in the final and decisive battle of the Texas revolution. In Houston's forces on the San Jacinto River were the surgeons Moses Albert Levy and Isaac Lyons. Other Jews under Houston's command were Major Leon Dyer, Levi Myers Harby of Charleston, Lieutenant Henry Seligson, and Albert Emanuel. San Jacinto freed Texas from Mexico, and for nearly ten years the Republic of Texas flew the Lone Star flag.

David Camden de Leon, a Charleston Jew, was a hero of the Mexican War and later the surgeon general of the Confederate army. (*American Jewish Archives, Cincinnati*)

Harris Kempner, Jewish pioneer and banker in nineteenth-century Texas. (*American Jewish Archives, Cincinnati*)

Austin secured a grant from the local Mexican authorities to bring American settlers into Texas. The rapid colonization of Texas had begun, as did political turmoil. Mexico, understandably fearful of American encroachment, restricted immigration, brought a strong military force into the province, tried to disarm the American settlers, and arrested Stephen Austin. Angry and dismayed, the American colonists fought back, and at a convention held in March 1836 Texas declared its independence from Mexico. The Texas revolution was in full swing. A large Mexican force was sent to subdue the rebels, some of whom had gathered at the Alamo, a mission in San Antonio. Several

In 1843 Sam Houston, then president of Texas, invited Henry Castro, a French Jew of dubious ancestry, to colonize the infant republic. Castro, who fancied himself Henri, comte de Castro, was successful, and several thousand Alsatians migrated to Texas. French titles impressed the Texans, and today the picturesque town of Castroville west of San Antonio preserves the name of le comte de Castro. David Kaufman, who gave his name to a Texas county and city, was a Jewish veteran of the Battle of Neches. He served in both houses of the Texas legislature, and when the Lone Star was joined to the Stars and Stripes, Kaufman was elected to the Congress. In the legislature, too, was Adolphus Sterne, a fighter for Texas independence from 1826 on. Barely able to support itself as a new republic, Texas for the most part longed for unification with the United States, and in 1845 Washington obliged. War between Mexico and the United States became inevitable. Manifest destiny moved ever westward.

In 1846, a year after Texas had joined the Union, President James Polk and Congress declared war on Mexican aggression, an aggression largely provoked by the American government. It was a short and violent war, ranging in distance from Brownsville, Texas, to Mexico City itself. Contingents of Jews fought in the American army; they included a company from Baltimore under the command of Samuel Goldsmith, Joseph Simpson, and Levi Benjamin.

From South Carolina came David Camden de Leon, the most colorful Jewish soldier of the Mexican War. A surgeon, de Leon often laid aside his scalpel to take up a saber, and at the Battle of Chapultepec, which opened the way to Mexico City, "the fighting doctor" twice led cavalry charges against the Mexican army. In 1861 he left the U.S. Army to become surgeon general of the Confederate forces.

When the Mexican War ended in 1848, the United States took control of all Mexican territory north of the Rio Grande, enlarging the state of Texas and giving us New Mexico, Arizona, and most of California, Colorado, and Utah; the last was to be the "gathering place for Israel," according to the Mormon Scriptures.

Philip Drachman, an American Jew, was among the earliest pioneers in Arizona. (*American Jewish Archives, Cincinnati*)

Columbus Moise, of the well-known Charleston family, was the chief justice of the New Mexico Territory in the nineteenth century. (*American Jewish Archives, Cincinnati*)

Isadore Elkan Solomon, founder of Solomon, Arizona, at his banking office in the 1870s. (*American Jewish Archives, Cincinnati*)

Mexico had lost two-fifths of its land, and America now stretched from sea to shining sea.

Just months after the Mexican War gold was discovered in California, and adventurers and fortune hunters from America and every other quarter of the world swarmed into the land of sunshine and gold, irresistibly drawn by the allure of yellow metal. Long, hazardous journeys through Indian lands, across desert wastes, and over storm-tossed oceans did not daunt the hardy, if gold-crazed, forty-niners. San Francisco, a quiet Mexican town, quickly became a brawling, booming city, the Golden Gate to fabulous riches. Even writers such as Bret Harte and Mark Twain were attracted to the roaring port, the Barbary Coast of which became infamous.

Joshua Abraham Norton, one of many Jewish forty-niners, arrived in San Francisco in November 1849 and viewed the sprawling scene with a fine eye for adventure. Tall, well built, and attractive, Norton had been born in London and enjoyed the manners of an English gentleman, which were to serve him well in the boorish society of early San Francisco. At age thirty, he had already adventured in South Africa with his father, John Norton, one of the founders of Port Elizabeth. Now California stood before him.

In the commercial chaos of San Francisco, where an item sold for 10 cents one day, $10 the next, and 5 cents on the following, depending on the daily status of gold, fortunes were made and lost overnight. It was the ideal oppor-

San Francisco, during the gold rush, attracted many Jewish forty-niners. (*The New York Public Library*)

tunity for a shrewd, bold trader who savored risk, and Norton was such a person. He plunged into the perilous market with joy, buying and selling commodities and speculating in gold mines and real estate. At one time his realty holdings were so extensive even he did not know all he owned. From his building on Montgomery Street, the center of the business district, Norton amassed a fortune, and by 1853 he was a major commercial factor in the life of the city. And then disaster struck. A fiery holocaust swept San Francisco, and the wooden city was virtually destroyed. Norton was financially ruined and began to exhibit extravagant behavior. For five years he vanished from the Bay City, and when he returned in 1859, he issued a formal proclamation to astonished and amused San Franciscans declaring himself "Norton I, Emperor of the United States."

Well remembered and well liked, Emperor Norton conquered San Francisco with his stately carriage and courtly manner. It troubled neither him nor his loyal subjects of San Francisco that the emperor was completely impoverished. Lodgings were provided for him at the Eureka Hotel by public largess. When hungry, he dined at any hotel, restaurant, or saloon as an honored guest; a bill was never proffered. He was a welcomed visitor at theaters, concert halls, and lectures, where he often debated the speakers with regal eloquence, much to the joy of the audience. Whenever he was in need of cash—and that was not often—he drew a check

upon any bank in San Francisco, and it was always honored despite his not having a penny in the bank. His splendid wardrobe was furnished by his subjects, and on ceremonial occasions he was a glory to behold in his military navy blue coat, trimmed with large gold epaulets and brass buttons, and his beaver top hat, decorated with a rosette and bright plumes. A lapel flower, a silk handkerchief dangling from his breast pocket, and an imperial sword completed his costume. While seemingly a figure of fun, Joshua Abraham Norton had captured the heart and imagination of San Francisco.

The emperor's many proclamations were given wide publicity in the local press and delighted his people. In one such he abolished the United States government "in order to save the nation from utter ruin and disgrace." After reigning for more than two decades, Emperor Norton died at sixty-one. Thirty thousand mourners attended the public funeral, the largest ever held in the Bay Area.

Levi Strauss, the creator of blue jeans, was another Jewish forty-niner but one quite different from the eccentric Norton. A New York peddler, Strauss caught gold fever, packed his few belongings, and bought passage on a schooner that sailed around Cape Horn, then north to the Golden Gate. His dream of being a mineowner, which spurred him on the dangerous journey, was never realized. However, there were other, more dependable ways to make a living. He arrived in San Francisco with

Bret Harte, one of America's greatest storytellers, was a Jewish forty-niner and the grandson of Bernard Harte, Secretary of the New York Stock Exchange in the early nineteenth century. (*American Jewish Archives, Cincinnati*)

Portrait of a weary emperor. (*American Jewish Archives, Cincinnati*)

his bolts of cloth and his packs of needles and pins, string, and sewing thread. He sold his stock in no time and bought bolts of canvas for tents. When the miners told him they already had tents and what they really needed was strong pairs of pants, Strauss struck his own lode.

Strauss, the basic businessman, arranged for tailors to cut and sew his entire supply of canvas into pants the seams of which were reinforced with copper rivets. His pants became enormously popular among the miners, and he ordered special denim cloth from France, had it dyed blue, put a little tag on the manufactured pants, and thus was born a new word in the English language: Levi's. Today, more than a century after they were first introduced, Levi Strauss's blue jeans and denims still sell widely, both here and abroad.

The great tunnel builder Adolph Sutro was a German Jew who emigrated to the United States in 1850. A year later he was in gold-struck San Francisco. A youth of twenty, he had crossed the fever-ridden Isthmus of Panama to reach his destination, the Golden Gate. Unfortunately the gold boom was on the wane, and young Adolph, an engineer by training, was forced to open a tobacco shop in the boisterous city. He had struggled for nine years when news of the rich Comstock strike in Nevada reached him. Sutro quickly sold his business and left for the Sierra Nevada, where he tried to find work with the mining entrepreneurs but failed. Undaunted, Sutro opened a small mill near the Comstock Lode which extracted minerals from mine tailings and proved a success.

As a mill operator he often heard the complaints of Comstock miners about poor ventilation, underground floods, and conditions so hazardous as to threaten the fabulous output of Mount Davidson, the site of the lode. Sutro pondered the question and after long and hard calculation came up with a plan that would solve the difficulties. A giant tunnel, almost five miles long, would be dug parallel to the Comstock mines in Mount Davidson to provide ventilation, water drainage, and transportation for the miners. It was to be 1,600 feet below

Pottery figurine of another Jewish forty-niner, Emperor Norton I of San Francisco. (*American Jewish Archives, Cincinnati*)

the surface. For years Sutro, obsessed with his great tunnel, sought financing from banks, wealthy investors, and the government with little success. Finally, he appealed to the Nevada miners themselves, the people most vitally concerned, and they responded generously. Sutro invested his own funds, and an English bank unexpectedly offered the needed additional capital.

The construction of the tunnel began in October 1869 and was completed after ten years of sweaty, bloody toil. The then-famous Sutro Tunnel was hailed as a miracle of engineering. During this trying period Sutro found time to write a study on *The Mineral Resources of the United States*. Once the great tunnel project was finished, the promoter and driving force behind it lost interest. He sold his share in the Sutro Tunnel for $5 million and returned, a rich and famous man, to the city he loved, San Francisco.

There he invested in real estate, built a library that bears his name, a museum, and an aquarium, and left San Franciscans Sutro Park. He lived in a beautiful white mansion surrounded by vast flower gardens, atop a stunning cliff beside the Pacific. His fellow citizens showed their esteem when they elected him mayor in 1894. When Adolph Sutro died at sixty-eight, the rugged and resourceful venturer owned 10 percent of the city's land.

Solomon Nunes Carvalho, born in Charleston in 1815, was an artist and an explorer and mapmaker in the Far West. As a youth Carvalho, the scion of an old Jewish family, won art prizes in South Carolina for his portraits. His painting of *Moses on Mount Sinai* hung in Beth Elohim Synagogue, but was destroyed in the great fire of 1838, along with the temple itself, one of the oldest and finest in the United States. The gracious lines of the old synagogue can still be seen, however, in Carvalho's early drawings.

When he was thirty-eight, the adventurous Carvalho joined John C. Frémont's 1854 expedition to explore the Far West. As mapmaker, he and twenty-one other men of Frémont's party crossed the Rocky Mountains on foot, in the dead cold of winter. Later his maps were followed by trail bosses, wagon trains, and railroad builders on their way to California. In 1857 Solomon Carvalho described the hardships of the perilous journey in a classic work: *Incidents of Travel and Adventure in the Far West with Colonel Frémont's Last Expedition.* While in Los Angeles, Carvalho sought out the Jews there and

Joshua Abraham Norton was accorded front-page honors by San Francisco's leading newspaper. (*American Jewish Archives, Cincinnati*)

Levi Strauss, the Jewish forty-niner who made his fortune in blue jeans. (*American Jewish Archives, Cincinnati*)

Solomon Heydenfeldt, the Jewish forty-niner who rose to become a Supreme Court justice in California. (*American Jewish Archives, Cincinnati*)

Adolph Sutro, the Jewish forty-niner who became one of the world's most famous tunnel builders. The Sutro Tunnel saved the Comstock Lode in Nevada from flooding. (*American Jewish Archives, Cincinnati*)

A plaque marking the site of the first Jewish synagogue in Los Angeles. (*American Jewish Archives, Cincinnati*)

Los Angeles in 1855, a year after the first Jewish congregation was established; Solomon Nunes Carvalho visited there. (*The New York Public Library*)

Solomon Nunes Carvalho of Charleston, well-known Jewish artist and explorer of the West. (*American Jewish Archives, Cincinnati*)

helped them organize a Hebrew Benevolent Society for new arrivals, and in Salt Lake City he painted a portrait of his friend Brigham Young, leader of the Mormons. After a long and full life Solomon Nunes Carvalho died at seventy-nine.

THE 1850s are often called the German period in American Jewish history for the number of German and Austrian Jews who came to our shores in those years. It is often opposed snobbishly to the so-called Cossack period of the 1880s, when myriads of poor and uneducated Jews arrived from East Europe—from Poland, Russia, and Rumania. These are at best limited definitions, and no call to judgment, since all were the children of Abraham. German and East European Jews were here prior to the Revolution, remained here, fought in every war, and helped build this country, as did the Sephardim, the Iberian Jews, who settled here first.

In the years before 1848, when liberal revolutionary outbreaks swept Europe, Prince von Metternich and his oppressive Holy Alliance held sway. Riots in Vienna and Berlin forced Metternich, who had forbidden all revolutions, to flee for his life. The revolutionaries were placated by promises of democratic constitutions which were to remain unfulfilled. By 1850 the revolutions were crushed, and the forces of repression were in control again. In the aftermath of the German Revolution of 1848 thousands of German Jews sought out their lodestar of freedom, the United States. Antisemitism had reached new heights in Germany, and sadly the Jews were being scapegoated, again. Tertullian, a father of the Roman Church, wrote in the third century: "If the Tiber rose to the walls of the city, if the inundation of the Nile failed to give the fields enough water, if the heavens did not send rain, if an earthquake occurred, if famine threatened, if pestilence raged, the cry resounded: Throw the Christians to the lions!" It might have greatly troubled Tertullian to find that in subsequent centuries Christians were throwing Jews to the lions. Many of the new German Jewish immigrants fought in the Mexican War and were to serve, in both blue and gray, in the tragic Civil War. From a population of fewer than 6,000 in Revolutionary times the American Jews were to number almost 150,000 prior to the Civil War, largely as a result of the influx of German Jews.

AS JEWISH PIONEERS, settlers, and entrepreneurs spread out from the eastern seaboard, congregations appeared across the nation. In New York City the first Ashkenazic synagogue, B'nai Jeshurun, then on Elm Street, was consecrated in 1827; Emanu-El, now on Fifth Avenue and Sixty-fifth Street, was originally formed in 1845. Congregations were organized in Albany, Syracuse, Rochester, and Buffalo. By the 1840s and 1850s New Haven and Hartford had established congregations, as did Paterson and Elizabeth in New Jersey.

In Pennsylvania there was Philadelphia, of course, but in Easton, Pittsburgh, Wilkes-Barre, Harrisburg, and Lancaster Jews also gathered into congregations. Jewish collective life had burgeoned in Baltimore after passage of the Jew Bill of 1825, and by the 1860s there were several synagogues in the city by the Chesapeake. In Richmond, Virginia, before the Civil War three congregations were active, while in Wilming-

ton, North Carolina, a Jewish burial ground was purchased in 1852. South Carolina had its Charlestonian Jews, and before 1860 a congregation had been established in Columbia. In Georgia Jewish communities were organized in Augusta, Columbus, and Macon in the 1850s; Savannah, with its much older Jewish families, led the establishment.

The first congregation in Ohio was founded in 1824 in Cincinnati, then a near wilderness. As German Jews arrived in the 1840s, more and more congregations were formed, and synagogues built. Under Rabbi Isaac Mayer Wise, who organized the Union of American Hebrew Congregations and founded Hebrew

David Levy Yulee of Florida was probably the first Jew to sit in the U.S. Senate. Elected in 1845, Levy or Yulee, as he called himself, was the son of Mordecai Levy, a wealthy Sephardic Jew who bought 250,000 acres in central Florida from Spain in 1812. Levy County in Florida was named for the family. (*American Jewish Archives, Cincinnati*)

Sol Star, Jewish cattle baron in
Montana in the 1870s. (*American Jewish
Archives, Cincinnati*)

The Max Idelman House
in Cheyenne, Wyoming.
Idelman, a Jewish
cattleman, was among the
earliest settlers of the
territory. (*American Jewish
Archives, Cincinnati*)

Julius Meyer, a nineteenth-century Nebraska trader, enjoying his
friends and business associates the Pawnee Indians. (*American
Jewish Archives, Cincinnati*)

Adam Gimbel of Indiana, founder of a department store dynasty. (*American Jewish Archives, Cincinnati*)

Simon Lazarus, nineteenth-century Ohio merchant and another department store dynast. (*American Jewish Archives, Cincinnati*)

Julius Houseman, nineteenth-century U.S. congressman and the first Jewish settler in Grand Rapids, Michigan. (*American Jewish Archives, Cincinnati*)

The original Goldwater store in Prescott in the 1870s. The Goldwaters, of Jewish origin, were among the first families of Arizona. (*American Jewish Archives, Cincinnati*)

Union College, Cincinnati became the center of Reform Judaism in America. So great was its rabbinical reputation that in future years Cincinnati became known as Jerusalem West. In Cleveland a congregation was formed in 1839, and by 1860 there were congregations in Columbus, Dayton, and Akron. Chicago, which was not incorporated as a city until 1837, became the metropolis of the Middle West. Eight years later enough Jews had settled there for a burial ground to be purchased, and a short time after that congregation Anshe Maarab, the Men of the West, was born. The congregation was able to build a synagogue, which was dedicated in 1851. In the years to come, tens of thousands of Jewish immigrants settled in the Windy City, and Jewish culture and philanthropy became proverbial. In Indianapolis, Fort Wayne, Lafayette, and Evansville small congregations existed in the 1850s, and in Iowa the first congregation appeared in Keokuk in 1855.

Milwaukee saw Jewish settlement in the 1850s, and Detroit had its first Jewish congregation in 1850. In St. Louis Jews worshiped together for the first time in 1836, but the first synagogue was not built until 1859.

In Louisville, Kentucky, the first synagogue was erected in 1850, while in Mobile and Montgomery, Alabama, congregations were formed in 1844 and 1852 respectively. The great Judah Touro had established Jewish life in New Orleans in the 1820s, as we have noted. Houston, Galveston, and San Antonio had congregations in the 1850s. In California Jewish forty-niners met under a tent in San Francisco

Michael Reese, nineteenth-century Jewish philanthropist in Chicago. A hospital was named in his honor. (*American Jewish Archives, Cincinnati*)

THE JEWS' HOSPITAL IN NEW YORK.

Jews' Hospital in New York City in the 1850s. It is now the world-famous Mount Sinai Medical Center. (*American Jewish Archives, Cincinnati*)

in October 1849 to celebrate the High Holy Days. Within a few years many congregations had arisen in San Francisco, Stockton, and Sacramento. The first congregation in the Northwest was launched in Portland in 1858, a year before Oregon was admitted to the Union. There was, of course, Jewish pioneering throughout the land long before the formation of distant congregations. And it should be noted, perhaps with regret, that many American Jews of whatever origin—Iberian, German, or East European—showed little interest in congregational affairs but remained loyal as secular Jews.

Isaac Leeser, the champion of traditional Judaism in America, was a German Jew who emigrated to Richmond, Virginia, in 1824, at the age of eighteen. Five years later he was chosen as preacher of Mikveh Israel in Philadelphia. There he became deeply concerned with American Jews who were moving away from traditional Jewish law and ritual and with the Reform movement, which in his eyes threatened basic Jewish values. In the years to come Leeser became the rival and chief opponent of the younger Isaac Mayer Wise of Cincinnati, the leader of the Reform movement, the American Judaism of the future, as it was

Rabbi Isaac Leeser of Philadelphia, the proponent of Orthodox values in American Jewish life. (*American Jewish Archives, Cincinnati*)

Isaac Mayer Wise of Cincinnati, a pioneer of Reform Judaism and an outstanding nineteenth-century rabbi. He opposed the traditional views of Isaac Leeser. (*American Jewish Archives, Cincinnati*)

then called. Leeser and Wise, both brilliant men, for years debated the issue of American Jewry, publicly and in print, with little resolution. However, by the late nineteenth century Reform Judaism had made imposing gains. Traditional Judaism was reinforced in 1887, when the Jewish Theological Seminary, the bastion of conservative Jewry in America, was opened in New York City.

The first national Jewish organization to be formed in the United States, and still among the most important in its influence, was the Independent Order of B'nai B'rith, or the Sons of the Covenant. Led by Henry Jones and a dozen other German Jews of humble origin, the organization held its first meeting at a café on Essex Street, on Manhattan's Lower East Side, in 1843. The committee, gazing into the future, envisioned a Jewish fraternal order that would bring together in harmony the contentious factions in American Jewish life, the Reform and the traditional Jew, the German and the Pole, the Pole and the Rumanian, and the rich and the poor. Mutual self-help and philanthropy outside the synagogue were to be the primary

goals, but that noblest of ambitions the unification of American Jewry was never forgotten. By 1860 there were fifty B'nai B'rith lodges in the United States; they supported orphan homes, old people's homes, and hospitals and offered charity to the indigent. Later B'nai B'rith through its Anti-Defamation League became a potent force against the ever-present menace of antisemitism. In 1923 B'nai B'rith, then the largest Jewish fraternal order in America, began to establish Hillel societies on college and university campuses for the edification of Jewish students.

WHILE AMERICAN JEWS tried to set their religious and social differences aside in the age-old tradition that Jew must never fight Jew, at least publicly, war clouds hovered on the national horizon. Pro and antislavery forces had gathered in Congress to do political debate, and when that failed, war between North and South became inevitable. In October 1859 John Brown, an implacable abolitionist from Kansas and elsewhere, attacked and captured the

Henry Jones, the major founder of the B'nai B'rith organization, was born Heinrich Jonas in Hamburg in 1811. (*B'nai B'rith, Washington, D.C.*)

John Brown of Kansas, who saw himself as an instrument in the hand of God. (*The New York Public Library*)

Harpers Ferry at the time of John Brown's raid. (*American Jewish Archives, Cincinnati*)

The fanatic abolitionist John Brown as portrayed by the artist
John Steuart Curry. (*American Jewish Archives, Cincinnati*)

United States arsenal at Harpers Ferry, Virginia, where there would be sufficient weapons to arm a slave insurrection in the South. Among Brown's followers in Kansas were August Bondi of Vienna, Jacob Benjamin of Bohemia, and Theodore Weiner of Poland, recent Jewish immigrants from Europe. Moritz Pinner, another Jewish abolitionist in "bleeding Kansas," was the editor of the German-language *Kansas Post;* later Pinner was a delegate to the Republican convention of 1860, which nominated the awesome and tragic Abraham Lincoln to the presidency. Shortly after John Brown had captured Harpers Ferry, a little-known United States Army colonel, Robert E. Lee, retook the arsenal, and Brown was hanged by the government. Before his death Brown, accused of cold-blooded murder, asserted he was merely an instrument in the hand of God. The events at Harpers Ferry sent shock waves through the South, but in the North John Brown was regarded as a martyr to the abolitionist cause.

Southern Jews backed the proslavery forces of Dixie, while in the North Jews overwhelmingly favored the abolitionist movement. As early as 1853 antislavery vigilantes in Chicago, led by Michael Greenebaum, one of the earliest Jewish settlers in that city, freed a captured runaway slave. Bernhard Felsenthal of Chicago, the Reform rabbi of Congregation Sinai, was an outspoken critic of slavery. In Philadelphia, despite the objections of his board of trustees, Rabbi Sabato Morais, an Italian-born Jew, continued to praise Abraham Lincoln from his pulpit; later Morais became the head of Jewish Theological Seminary in New York. In Cincinnati Rabbi Max Lilienthal spoke out boldly

against slavery. Lewis Dembitz of Louisville, Kentucky, was one of the young Republicans who placed Lincoln in nomination at the convention of 1860. At twenty-eight he was a successful lawyer and prominent Jewish leader in that city; his nephew Louis Dembitz Brandeis was to become a Supreme Court justice.

In New York, however, one Jewish leader, Rabbi Morris Jacob Raphall of B'nai Jeshurun, came to the defense of slavery. After close study of the Scriptures he concluded that the Bible approved of slavery and preached a sermon condemning abolitionists, especially the clergyman Henry Ward Beecher. His sermon, which was carried in the press, was a shock

August Bondi of Kansas, one of John Brown's Jewish abolitionist supporters. (*American Jewish Archives, Cincinnati*)

Betty Kohn Wollman, Jewish pioneer in Kansas, was visited at her home in Leavenworth by Abraham Lincoln in 1859. (*American Jewish Archives, Cincinnati*)

Bernhard Felsenthal of Chicago, an ardent abolitionist. (*American Jewish Archives, Cincinnati*)

Max Lilienthal of Cincinnati, the outspoken critic of slavery. (*American Jewish Archives, Cincinnati*)

Sabato Morais, the Italian-born rabbi who continued to praise Abraham Lincoln from his pulpit in Philadelphia despite the objections of his congregation. (*American Jewish Archives, Cincinnati*)

to New York Jews and an instant sensation in the South, where pamphlets were printed promoting the good rabbi's biblical justification of slavery. In the North he was attacked by one and all, and in short order his moments of fame became days of notoriety when he was vilified as "the Hebrew defamer of the law of his nation" and the source of ideas "full of falsehood, nonsense and blasphemy." The biblical justification of slavery was to die, but it died hard.

David Einhorn, rabbi of Congregation Har Sinai in Baltimore, was a militant abolitionist in a Maryland torn by pro and antislavery mobs. From his pulpit and in his writings Einhorn preached the doctrine of antislavery, placing himself and his congregation, according to

Morris Jacob Raphall of New York, the foolish old rabbi who promoted a biblical defense of slavery. (*American Jewish Archives, Cincinnati*)

David Einhorn, the renowned abolitionist rabbi of Baltimore, who was several times threatened by angry proslavery mobs. (*American Jewish Archives, Cincinnati*)

them, in physical jeopardy. Courageous and bold, the rabbi refused to be silenced by his board of trustees. After several threats from extremists, young armed Jews took to guarding the synagogue and the home and family of Rabbi Einhorn. In April 1861, following four days of bloody rioting, the rabbi and his family reluctantly left Baltimore for Philadelphia, never again to return to the strife-torn city. Maryland suffered the classic pains of a border state but remained loyal to the Union.

With the election of Lincoln Southern planters, haunted by the prospect of the emancipation of their more than 2 million slaves, began to talk secession and even war. Before the debacle John C. Calhoun of South Carolina, the foremost spokesman of the South, claimed that "there cannot be a durable republic without slavery" and pointed to the civilizations of Greece and Rome, dear to the hearts of the Southern slaveowners. Cotton was king, and cotton planters needed slaves. The agricultural South and its wealth and economy were put at deep risk by Yankee moralists, who themselves were then initiating a new kind of industrial slavery in the North. Jewish planters, largely Sephardic in origin, shared the fears of

The Capitol as it looked on the morning of Lincoln's first inauguration in 1861. The dome was yet to be completed. (*Collection of Peter Quinn*)

President Abraham Lincoln, an awesome and tragic figure in American history. (*American Jewish Archives, Cincinnati*)

General Robert E. Lee's polite refusal to Rabbi Michelbacher, who had requested that Jewish Confederate soldiers be placed on leave for the High Holy Days. (*American Jewish Archives, Cincinnati*)

Maximilian Michelbacher, the Richmond rabbi and a fervent supporter of the Confederacy. (*American Jewish Archives, Cincinnati*)

other Southern slaveowners and stood side by side with the rich Southern gentry. Poor Southern Jews who fought for the Confederacy—and there were many—fought out of regional loyalty, not because they wished to protect the institution of slavery, an issue with as little meaning for them as for their Christian fellow rebels. Northern Jews, sincere believers in abolition and in the preservation of the Union, rallied around the flag. At about that time, too, Ashkenazic Jews, heavily outnumbering the aristocratic Sephardim, displaced them as leaders of Jewish America.

South Carolina left the Union in December 1860, the first Southern state to secede. Soon after, several other states joined South Carolina to form the Confederacy at Montgomery, Alabama, which for a short time was the capital of the secessionists. Richmond, because of its prestige, was to become the permanent capital of the Confederate government. The new government demanded federal property, especially forts and arsenals, within its domain. When President Lincoln refused to comply, Confederate forces bombarded Fort Sumter in Charleston Harbor on April 12, 1861, formally beginning the War Between the States, the bloodiest and most heartbreaking war in American history. At its peak more than 2.5 million Americans were locked in combat, and casualties soared well beyond the 700,000 mark. Historians of later times have characterized the war as a regional struggle without basic cause, an irrepressible conflict, or criminally stupid, an unnecessary bloodletting brought on by arrogant extremists and blundering politicians.

In Richmond Maximilian Michelbacher, one of the rabbinical leaders of Southern Jewry, composed a prayer for Jewish troopers in the

Simon Baruch, the father of Bernard Baruch, was reared in South Carolina, where he became a Confederate surgeon. After the Civil War he was appointed the first chief of medicine at Montefiore Hospital in New York. (*Montefiore Hospital and Medical Center, The Bronx*)

Edwin Warren Moise, a Charleston Moise, was a senior officer in the Confederate army. (*American Jewish Archives, Cincinnati*)

The Frauenthal family house in Conway, Arkansas. Max Frauenthal, the Confederate hero, was part of that distinguished Jewish brood. (*American Jewish Archives, Cincinnati*)

ranks of the gray, which declared in part: "Our f123 firesides are threatened" by a foe that intends "to desecrate our soil, to murder our people, and deprive us of the glorious inheritance . . . of this once great Republic." In the capital, too, was the *Richmond Examiner,* which published so many scurrilous lies aimed at Southern Jewry that Colonel Adolphus Adler of the Confederate army challenged its editor to a duel. The editor, a blowhard, as were many editors of the yellow-press, backed off. This was not to be the first or the last manifestation of redneck antisemitism, which at times became savage.

There were more than 5,000 Jews in the Confederate forces, and many of them distinguished themselves in battle. Max Frauenthal, "a little Jew" with "the heart of a lion," as a fellow trooper described him, plunged into combat with reckless abandon. So famous were his exploits that his name, corrupted to Fronthall, became a commendation for Confederate soldiers who displayed exceptional courage; they were known as "real Fronthalls." Max Ullman of Mississippi, another Jewish private, served through the whole war, was twice wounded, and, after hostilities had ended, became a rabbi in Birmingham, Alabama. Families of Southern Jews joined the ranks of the Confederacy: the five Moses brothers of South Carolina, the six Cohen brothers of North Carolina, the three Levy brothers of Louisiana, and the three Levy brothers of Virginia. Many of them were to die in combat. Lieutenant Albert Luria died a hero at the Battle of Fair Oaks, near Richmond, and Marx Cohen in the Battle of Bentonville, near Goldsboro, North Carolina.

E. J. Levy, Confederate captain of the Richmond Light Infantry Blues in the Civil War. (*American Jewish Archives, Cincinnati*)

DEDICATED TO
JOSEPH G. SWIFT
AND
SIMON M. LEVY
COMPRISING THE FIRST CLASS TO GRADUATE
FROM THE U.S. MILITARY ACADEMY
12 OCTOBER 1802
"YOU SHOWED US THE WAY
THE LONG GRAY LINE FOLLOWS
IN DUTY, IN HONOR AND FOR COUNTRY."

PRESENTED ON THE OCCASION OF THE
AMERICAN JEWISH TERCENTENARY
6 MARCH 1955

The plaque at West Point honoring the academy's first two
graduates in 1802. Simon Levy, a Baltimore soldier, was a hero
of the Battle of Fallen Timbers in Ohio. (*U.S. Military Academy*)

Adolph Proskauer, a Jewish banker, was promoted to major after being wounded four times.

In the higher ranks of the Confederacy were David Camden de Leon, the saber-wielding surgeon of the Mexican War who became surgeon general of the Southern forces; Levi Myers Harby, another hero of the Mexican War, who was in command of Galveston, a major Confederate port; Lionel Levy, the judge advocate of the Military Court; and Abraham Myers, the quartermaster general and a West Point graduate.

In October 1802 the newly founded United States Military Academy at West Point held its first graduation exercises, and two cadets,

one Simon Magruder Levy, Jewish and the other Christian, were graduated as lieutenants, the only ones to be so commissioned in a corps of ten. Levy, the son of a prominent Baltimore Jew, had been appointed a cadet for his heroism at the Battle of Fallen Timbers in August 1794, when Anthony Wayne decisively defeated an Indian confederation at the Maumee Rapids near present-day Toledo. Lieutenant Levy was the first Jewish officer to be commissioned by the academy. Many American Jews were to follow. They included Samuel Noah, West Point's thirtieth graduate, who joined a military unit defending Brooklyn during the War of 1812; for many years Noah, who died at ninety-two,

NEGROES, NEGROES.

The undersigned has just arrived in Lumpkin from Virginia, with a likely lot of negroes, about 40 in number, embracing every shade and variety. He has seamstresses, chamber maids, field hands, and doubts not that he is able to fill the bill of any who may want to buy. He has sold over two hundred negroes in this section, mostly in this county, and flatters himself that he has so far given satisfaction to his purchasers. Being a regular trader to this market he has nothing to gain by misrepresentation, and will, therefore, warrant every negro sold to come up to the bill, squarely and completely. Give him a call at his Mart.

J. F. MOSES.

Lumpkin, Ga., Nov. 14th, 1859.

Rare handbill advertising the wares of a Jewish slave dealer. (*American Jewish Archives, Cincinnati*)

Senator Judah P. Benjamin of Louisiana, the brilliant advocate of slavery and a slaveowner himself. (*Collection of Peter Quinn*)

was the academy's oldest living graduate. In 1983 groundbreaking ceremonies for an impressive Jewish chapel at West Point, the first such chapel in the United States, took place. During the terrible days of the Civil War many West Pointers, Robert E. Lee, Stonewall Jackson, and Ulysses S. Grant, to name a few, would find themselves on opposing firing lines.

By far the most outstanding Jew in the Confederacy was Judah Philip Benjamin of Louisiana, who as attorney general, secretary of war, and secretary of state became the most influential political force in Dixie, after Jefferson Davis and General Robert E. Lee. President Davis found Benjamin indispensable: "the brains of the Confederacy," he was called in the North.

Born on St. Croix, the Virgin Islands, in 1811, the infant Benjamin and his Sephardic parents migrated to Wilmington, North Carolina, and thence to Charleston, South Carolina, where they settled. A precocious youth, he entered Yale at fourteen, and although he was never graduated, young Benjamin is still considered one of the college's most distinguished students. When he was seventeen, Benjamin moved to New Orleans, where he found work with a notary and studied French and the law in his spare time; four years later he was admitted to the Louisiana bar. His reputation as a

Judah P. Benjamin, as secretary of war for the Confederacy. Cries of "Kill the Jew!" resounded through Dixie after the defeat of Southern military forces. (*American Jewish Archives, Cincinnati*)

bright young lawyer soon earned him a large practice, which made him rich enough to become a sugar planter and slaveowner as well.

Passionate about politics, especially Southern politics, he served in both houses of the Louisiana legislature and in 1852 was elected to the United States Senate, one of the first Jews to serve in that august body. In the Senate, Benjamin, who was regarded by many Northern senators as "an Israelite with an Egyptian heart," was a brilliant defender of the system of slavery. His talent as a jurist was so widely acknowledged that he was once tendered the high office of Supreme Court justice. Like many Southerners, Benjamin resisted secession, but when the Confederacy was formed, he joined the exodus of Southern statesmen from Washington. He became the most trusted adviser to Jefferson Davis, his friend and colleague from Senate days. A tireless, able, and bold administrator, Benjamin, the Jew, was to be blamed for every Southern defeat. On the collapse of the Confederacy in 1865 Judah Benjamin, one of the South's staunchest advocates, was made the scapegoat. Cries of "Kill the Jew!" and destroy "that Judas" resounded through Dixieland. To escape the wrath of his enemies, and there seemed to have been more in the South than in the North, Benjamin, the statesman of a lost cause, surreptitiously made his way through Tampa, Florida, and the West Indies to London. There, more than fifty years old and almost penniless, he carved out a second career in law. He won immediate recognition with his *A Treatise on the Law of Sale of Personal Property*, published in 1868 and still held to be a classic. Enjoying the support of both Benjamin Disraeli and William Gladstone, Judah Benjamin became one of the leading barristers of England. When he died at seventy-three, the indomitable Louisianian, universally acknowledged to have been in the front rank of his profession, still believed in slavery. His ties to Judaism were tenuous, but he never converted, despite fierce pressure from his peers in the South and in London and from his wife, a Catholic Creole. In 1884 he was buried in Paris, bringing to a close the strange and fascinating history of Judah Philip Benjamin.

Adah Isaacs Menken, the most popular dancer of her time, shortly before her death. (*American Jewish Archives, Cincinnati*)

Life goes on even in the midst of war. In vivid contrast to Judah Benjamin was Adah Isaacs Menken, a fellow Louisianian who was to become the dancing sensation of her time. Born of Sephardic parents, near New Orleans in 1835, Adah fancied herself at times as Dolores Adios Fuertes. Her first great success was in the title role of Byron's *Mazeppa*, which was performed in San Francisco in 1863. From there to New York, London, and Paris she rebelled against social conventions with her daring, uninhibited, and provocative dancing. A dazzling beauty, she was adored by the high and mighty and despised by their wives. For several years she was the widely acclaimed toast of America and Europe, an international celebrity, the friend of Henry Wadsworth Longfellow and Alexandre Dumas and the royal families of Europe. Unfortunately she became ill and could no longer dance. Her celebrity was gone, as were her friends. She died in abject poverty in Paris with a rabbi at her bedside, ending a brief but fabulous career. The enchanting Adah was thirty-three years old.

IN THE NORTH, where there were some 7,000 American Jews under arms, 10 Jews held the rank of general. Frederick Knefler, a major general, was the highest-ranking Jew in the Union army. Born in Hungary, the young Knefler migrated to Indianapolis in the 1850s. When the war broke out, he volunteered as a private in an Indiana regiment and rose to be regimental colonel, marking the beginning of a stunning military career. He took part in the major battles fought by the Army of the Cumberland and served under Generals William S. Rosecrans and Ulysses S. Grant. After the Battle of Chickamauga in Tennessee, Knefler was promoted to major general for his heroic conduct. A year later he rode with General William T. Sherman in his historic and devastating march through Georgia.

Brigadier General Alfred Mordecai was to become one of the foremost ordnance experts in the United States Army in the last half of the nineteenth century. After graduation from West Point in 1861, he joined the Army of Northeastern Virginia, and received high commendation for his conduct at the Battle of Bull Run. Mordecai served as chief ordnance officer in several Union regiments, and in 1865 he was appointed instructor of ordnance and gunnery at the Military Academy.

Edward S. Salomon was born in Schleswig, Germany, in 1836, the eldest of eleven children in a family of well-to-do Jews. Educated and intelligent, young Salomon took a lively interest in the Revolutions of 1848 and in military

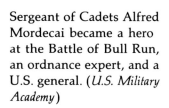

Sergeant of Cadets Alfred Mordecai became a hero at the Battle of Bull Run, an ordnance expert, and a U.S. general. (*U.S. Military Academy*)

Frederick Knefler, the young Jewish immigrant from Hungary whose stunning military successes in the Civil War raised him from private to major general of the Union army. (*American Jewish Archives, Cincinnati*)

General Edward Salomon, hero of Cemetery Ridge, who was appointed governor of the Washington Territory in 1870. (*American Jewish Archives, Cincinnati*)

At the Battle of Gettysburg many Jewish soldiers, including the great Edward Salomon, distinguished themselves. (*American Jewish Archives, Cincinnati*)

studies. Like many other German Jewish youths of his generation, who found the political situation in Germany intolerable, he migrated to the land of freedom. At seventeen he was in New York and after that in Chicago, where he held a variety of odd jobs until he became the clerk to a local justice of the peace. His study of law commenced there, and at twenty-three he was admitted to the Illinois bar. A year later he was elected to the Chicago City Council, with the backing of Lincoln's Republican party, the party of young men.

On the outbreak of the Civil War, Salomon, then twenty-five, was commissioned a second lieutenant in the first call for troops. He won quick promotions to major and finally became lieutenant colonel of a new regiment, the Eighty-second Illinois Infantry, recruited from Chicago's Jews, Poles, Hungarians, and Germans, the so-called foreign element. As-

signed to the Army of the Potomac, Salomon's troops fought with distinction at Chancellorsville and in several other battles before Gettysburg. As proven veterans they were joined to the great Union army assembling around Gettysburg, in preparation for the battle that would be the turning point of the Civil War.

In June 1863 General Lee, with 70,000 men, flushed with victories at Fredericksburg and Chancellorsville, sought to relieve pressure on the South by an invasion of Maryland and Pennsylvania. Lee aimed a blow at the heart of the Union defense, gambling on a quick thrust to wrest a surrender on Northern soil. General George G. Meade, commander of the Army of the Potomac, decided to make his stand against the Confederate incursion at the village of Gettysburg, Pennsylvania. He placed his army of 100,000 in a strong position and waited. On July 1 the two great armies met,

Colonel Marcus Spiegel, the son of an Ohio rabbi, was killed in battle before the papers promoting him to general were issued. (*American Jewish Archives, Cincinnati*)

and the fighting was fierce and bloody. The Eleventh Corps, of which Colonel Salomon's regiment was a part, bore the brunt of the attack on Cemetery Ridge, and for more than two days and nights Salomon and his immigrant soldiers held the line, despite heavy and constant fire and vicious hand-to-hand combat. Half his regiment was lost, and he himself narrowly escaped death several times. On July 4 Lee began his retreat, and victory rested with the Union forces. Some 40,000 were killed in this, the bloodiest battle of the war. Salomon received a special commendation from General Carl Schurz for "displaying the highest order of coolness and determination under very trying circumstances."

After Gettysburg, Colonel Salomon campaigned in Tennessee, Georgia, and the Carolinas under Generals Grant, Hooker, and Sherman. In 1865, after several more commendations for gallantry under fire, Salomon was promoted to brigadier general by Secretary of

War Edwin M. Stanton. General Salomon was twenty-nine years old.

He returned to Chicago after the war and was elected clerk of Cook County, a position he held for four years. On his thirty-third birthday General Salomon was appointed territorial governor of Washington by his friend President Grant, whom he served for one term. Salomon then moved to San Francisco, where he resumed his political career as district attorney and as the ablest speaker in the California legislature. In 1913, at the age of seventy-seven, Edward Salomon, one of the most distinguished soldiers of his time, died in San Francisco.

Leopold Blumenberg, one of the few Jewish officers in the Prussian Army, emigrated to the United States in 1854. In Baltimore he joined the congregation of the abolitionist Rabbi David Einhorn and was almost lynched by a proslavery mob. When the South bombarded Fort Sumter, he left a promising business career to enlist in the Union forces. As a major he helped organize the Fifth Maryland Regiment, which served with distinction in the Peninsular campaign and at the fierce Battle of Antietam. Blumenberg, by then a colonel, was severely wounded and was confined to bed for months. He never fully recovered. Lincoln appointed the crippled Blumenberg provost marshal of the Third Maryland District, and President Andrew Johnson elevated him to the rank of brigadier general.

Philip Joachimsen, who commanded a New York regiment, was another Jewish brigadier general. As United States attorney in New York he prosecuted and won many convictions against slave traders. In later life he played an important role in the organizing of Jewish philanthropies. Marcus Spiegel, the son of a rabbi, led an Ohio regiment into battle but was killed before his promotion to general was issued. Leopold Newman, the colonel of a New York regiment, was mortally wounded at the Battle of Chancellorsville, but before Newman died, President Lincoln visited him and promoted him to brigadier general. Max Einstein, a brigadier general in the Pennsylvania militia, distinguished himself at the first Battle of Bull Run when his regiment successfully covered the retreat of the Union army. Cameron's Dragoons, a Pennsylvania cavalry regiment, with a large proportion of Jews, was headed by the staunch Max Friedman. The surgeon general of the North was Phineas Jonathan Horwitz, a Jew, as was his opposite number in the South.

In July 1864 Congress authorized the award of the Congressional Medal of Honor, the highest decoration for valor that can be given to an American soldier and the most difficult to win. Seven Jews—Leopold Karpeles, Abraham Cohn, Isaac Gans, Abraham Grunwalt, Henry Heller, Benjamin Levy, and David Urbansky—all enlisted men, were among the first soldiers ever to be so honored. Karpeles, the color sergeant of the Fifty-seventh Massachusetts Infantry, saved part of the Union army at the Battle of the Wilderness, near Fredericksburg, by rallying retreating Union troops around his colors and persuading them to stand fast. Born in Prague, Karpeles became a Texan by adoption but journeyed north to join the

Dr. Phineas Jonathan Horwitz, surgeon general of the Union forces in the Civil War. (*American Jewish Archives, Cincinnati*)

Captain Michael Allen of Philadelphia, unofficial rabbi of Cameron's Dragoons in the Civil War. (*American Jewish Archives, Cincinnati*)

Color Sergeant Leopold
Karpeles, born in Prague,
reared in Texas, and
winner of the Congres-
sional Medal of Honor
for his bravery at the
Battle of the Wilderness.
(*American Jewish Archives,
Cincinnati*)

Isaac Moses of New York City, an
adjutant general of militia in the Civil
War. (*American Jewish Archives,
Cincinnati*)

Abraham Cohn, winner
of the Congressional
Medal of Honor in the
Civil War, was a member
of the Sixty-eighth New
York Volunteers.
(*American Jewish Archives,
Cincinnati*)

Color Sergeant Benjamin
Levy of the Fortieth New
York Infantry, winner of
the Congressional Medal
of Honor in the Civil War.
(*American Jewish Archives,
Cincinnati*)

Union forces in Massachusetts when the war broke out. Abraham Cohn was another hero of the Battle of the Wilderness; Grunwalt captured the Confederate flag at Franklin, Tennessee; while Urbansky showed extraordinary courage at the battles of Shiloh and Vicksburg and Levy rescued a Union warship from capture at the risk of his life.

Their distinguished record in the Civil War availed the Jews little in their continuing struggle against antisemitism, even in the North. The spirit of the Know-Nothing party, the spirit of bigotry, of anti-Catholicism, and antisemitism, marched on, as it does today. In the United States Senate Henry Wilson of Massachusetts made frequent references to "Jew brokers" and to those who had "crucified the Redeemer of the world." Benjamin Franklin Butler, an incompetent Union general, was an implacable Jew hater. A notorious failure in battle, General Butler in later life was elected governor of Massachusetts. William Gannaway Brownlow, a Methodist preacher from Tennessee, toured the North and drew large crowds

Richmond, the capital of the Confederacy, after General Grant's victory there. The photograph was taken in 1865 by the little-known firm of Levy and Cohen. (*American Jewish Archives, Cincinnati*)

with his rabid, rabble-rousing performances. After the war he became governor of Tennessee, a state he almost ruined with his harsh measures of Reconstruction. The American people as a whole were not antisemitic, but hard times bring hard prejudice.

In the second year of the war General Ulysses S. Grant issued the infamous General Order No. 11, which ordered all Jewish traders to leave the vast area under his command: "The Jews, as a class violating every regulation of trade established by the Treasury Department and also department orders, are hereby expelled from the department within twenty-four hours from the receipt of this order." Within twenty-four hours, however, President Lincoln, who had many Jewish friends, telegraphed the following message to Grant: "A paper purporting to be General Orders No. 11, issued by you December 17, has been presented here. By its

terms, it throws out all Jews from your department. If such an order has been sent out, it will immediately be revoked." Grant, knowing by then that he had been manipulated by slanderous Christian merchants seeking to drive Jews out of business, denied knowledge of Order No. 11.

On April 9, 1865, the bloodiest war in our history came to an end with the quiet surrender of Robert E. Lee to U. S. Grant at the Appomattox Courthouse in Virginia. Six days later Lincoln was assassinated by a half-mad Southern fanatic. The death of the president, a titanic figure in American history, partially closed the wounds of the Civil War, yet to be fully healed. Jews across the nation gathered in synagogues to mourn the loss of the martyred champion of human rights, rights that for so long had been denied in other lands and were therefore to be cherished.

PART FIVE

◀ The hurly-burly of Wall Street, the financial
center of our country, as it looked in 1845. The
financial district was to burgeon after the Civil
War. (*J. & W. Seligman & Co.*)

The Jewish
Establishment

PRIOR TO THE CIVIL WAR a gentile social establishment
arose in New York. It included the Morrises and Van Rensse-
laers, the Astors and Vanderbilts, the self-proclaimed first
families of America, the leading lights of the future Four Hundred.
Wealthy and powerful, chic and exclusive, vulgar and arrogant,
they were to dominate the American social scene for decades.
The Four Hundred, the makers of the *Social Register,* sought nothing
less than to emulate, and to excel, the pretensions of the English
aristocracy, their social betters. In pretensions they were a bounc-
ing success; in taste and tradition, a dismal failure.

The Jewish establishment in New York, which at its zenith
thoughtlessly mirrored the snobby chic of the gentile Four Hundred, *their* social betters, was to become known as the One Hundred or "our crowd," as termed by the modern writer Stephen
Birmingham. The Seligmans, Guggenheims, Loebs, Lehmans, and
Schiffs, German Jews associated with Wall Street, financial grand
dukes all, matched the gentile establishment dollar for dollar.
While this game of challenge was going on, tens of thousands
of poor Jewish immigrants were swarming into the dank tenements
of the Lower East Side with little more than hope in their pockets.

Horatio Alger, the writer of boys' stories, published his
first book in 1867 at the peak of the post-Civil War boom, when,
according to Alger, wealth and honor would come to anyone who
led an exemplary life and struggled valiantly against poverty and
other odds. In more than 100 books his rags-to-riches stories in-

J. Pierpont Morgan, the king of Wall Street, directing his royal
ire against a photographer. Morgan's chauffeur is forcibly
restraining the great man. The Seligmans and other Jewish bankers
on the Street dealt gingerly with old J. P. (*Library of Congress*)

spired the American poor to greater efforts on
behalf of the established rich, an approach to
work that did not displease the bankers and
the mill and factory owners of the North. In
the South, where the land lay like a corpse,
the simpleminded homilies of Horatio Alger
bore few crops. The postwar boom flattened
out, and financial and industrial disaster shook
the country through the Panic of 1873, with
an appalling number of business failures and
railroad and bank defaults, followed by a sharp
depression. The hardworking poor, both Jew
and Christian, were going from rags to rags
while the rich went to dinner parties. The Alger
theorem, which had become part of the Ameri-

can character and dream, was discredited, but
only for a time; in subsequent years the politics
of the rich was to focus on the poor as failures
in their struggle against poverty and thus deserving of their fate. If only the poor worked
harder, there would be no needy in America,
a point of view still cherished among the
wealthy.

J. Pierpont Morgan, the most powerful
banker of his time and the king of the gentile
financial establishment, precipitated the disas-
trous Panic of 1873 through his ruthless machi-
nations. The son of a successful banker, Morgan went from riches to more riches by dint
of a rapacious appetite. Old J. P. Morgan had

Joseph Seligman, from peddler in Pennsylvania to world banker,
a true American success story. (*J. & W. Seligman & Co.*)

no need for Horatio Alger. Morgan's rival on Wall Street was the banker Joseph Seligman, the king of "our crowd" and often the target of directed antisemitism. The life of Seligman, unlike Morgan's, provides us with an American success story that would warm the pen of Horatio Alger and did.

Born in Baiersdorf, Bavaria, in 1819, young Joseph Seligman was to rise from immigrant peddler to founder of an international banking house of vast importance, J. & W. Seligman & Company, and the financial adviser to the president of the United States. He and his seven brothers became the preeminent Jewish family in the country and were referred to as the American Rothschilds. All this from the humblest of beginnings.

Seligman was born on "Jew Street" in Baiersdorf, the first child of the village weaver; ten children were to follow, stretching the family resources from modest to nil. Nonetheless his mother, Fanny, had dreams for her firstborn, dreams of America and dreams of an education, in the best tradition of Jewish mothers. Somehow she raised enough money to send the fourteen-year-old boy to the University of Erlangen, where he was a brilliant student, despite constant baiting by his German classmates. At the university he studied literature and the classics, and when he left, after two years, he delivered his farewell oration in Greek; he already had command of German, Hebrew, Yiddish, English, and French.

At seventeen Seligman decided to emigrate to America, and with little more than passage money, arranged by his mother, and strict admonitions from his father to observe the Sabbath and the dietary laws, he left Baiersdorf. The crossing took nine weeks, during which time young Seligman slept on a filthy wooden plank in steerage, an experience he never forgot. Arriving in New York in a weakened condition, he set out almost immediately for Mauch Chunk, Pennsylvania, where he had a distant cousin; the future banker hiked for more than 100 miles on foot to get to that unattractive coal-mining settlement. In Mauch Chunk he met Asa Packer, a Connecticut Yankee who built coal barges and was the town's leading citizen. Packer instantly took to the bright Jewish immigrant and hired him as cashier-clerk, establishing a friendship that lasted for years. From a small-town businessman, Packer was to become a multimillionaire, the founder of Lehigh University, and the president of the Lehigh Valley Railroad—a good friend for Seligman to have.

The young Seligman, eager to have his own business, reluctantly left his friend Packer for greener fields. He became a foot peddler in rural Pennsylvania. Within six months he had saved enough money to send for his brothers William and James, still in Baiersdorf, and within months the three Seligmans were tramping through the countryside, selling their wares. By 1840 the Seligman boys had made enough to rent a small building in Lancaster, which served as headquarters for their peddling enterprises and where they could sleep in beds, a luxury

Ulysses S. Grant, in later years, showing the strains of the Civil War, the presidency, and illness. Grant, one of the most human of American leaders, presented this portrait of himself to the Seligmans. (*J. & W. Seligman & Co.*)

Horatio Alger, tutor to the Seligman children, was America's most prolific and edifying novelist. His rags-to-riches stories became part of the American dream. Alger himself was anything but a red-blooded American boy-hero. (*J. & W. Seligman & Co.*)

for a pack peddler. Their brother Jesse was sent for, and the fourteen-year-old was placed in charge of headquarters. Gradually the Seligmans left foot-peddling for greater rewards as town merchants. Joseph, the master of his younger brothers and a stickler for cost efficiency, once shouted at his brother James, who had the temerity to request a horse and wagon for his peddling activities: "What do I say? I say *chutzpah!* Horse and wagon indeed! Why did God give you feet?"

By 1843 the Seligmans had left Pennsylvania for Alabama, where they continued their profitable merchandising operations. By the same year Joseph had brought from Germany the rest of the family—all except Fanny, who had died the year before—and had them safely settled on Grand Street on the Lower East Side of New York City. In Pennsylvania and Ala-

bama the Seligman brothers usually suffered the frequent pain of antisemitic slurs and jeers in silence, but in bigoted Selma, Joseph struck an Alabamian antisemite and narrowly escaped a prison sentence. The Seligmans were happy in the knowledge that their younger brothers and sisters and their father were living in New York.

In the ensuing years the brothers opened stores in New York and St. Louis, in several Southern towns, and in less prepossessing places such as Watertown, New York. In distant Watertown the Seligmans acquired a very valuable friend, the young, hard-drinking First Lieutenant Ulysses S. Grant, who was then stationed at nearby Madison Barracks.

Joseph Seligman, who had set up this far-flung operation, was still under thirty and in need of a wife. In 1848 he found the lovely

William Seligman, the most snobbish of the Seligman brothers, who wished to change the name of the firm because it sounded too Jewish. (*J. & W. Seligman & Co.*)

Jesse Seligman, who struck it rich in San Francisco. (*J. & W. Seligman & Co.*)

Babet Steinhart while on a trip to Baiersdorf, Germany. The newly married couple settled in New York, where Joseph's store on William Street was to become One William Street, the site of an ornate eleven-story building, headquarters of J. & W. Seligman & Company. Jesse Seligman, the bookkeeper of their hard days in Lancaster, had struck it rich in California. A forty-niner, he had opened a general store in San Francisco and begun to trade and buy gold bars, a commerce that was to make the firm of Seligman an immense fortune and the foremost German Jewish bankers in the United States. Through the many ironies of Wall Street, One William Street later became the House of Lehman Brothers, rivals of the Seligmans.

During the Civil War J. & W. Seligman & Company established itself as one of the outstanding American banking firms, with foreign branches in Germany, Britain, and France. When the federal government most needed financial support in the dark days of the war,

it was the Seligmans who sold $200 million in United States bonds to European investors. After the war the Seligmans were appointed fiscal agents to the government, and when Grant became president, he offered the office of secretary of the treasury to his longtime friend Joseph Seligman, but the banker declined.

The Seligmans, Joseph and Babet, lived happily in a large Manhattan brownstone with their many children and their tutor, Horatio Alger. The Seligman brothers, led by Joseph, had a powerful drive for Americanization, even in the earliest days when first names changed quickly: James had been born Jacob; Jesse was Isaias; William was Wolf; Henry was Hermann; and Leopold was Lippmann. However, Joseph drew the line at one family name change: Once William, the most snobbish of the Seligmans, journeyed from Paris to confront his eldest brother with the demand that "now that we are men of substance, I suggest that we change our name." Joseph leaned back for a moment

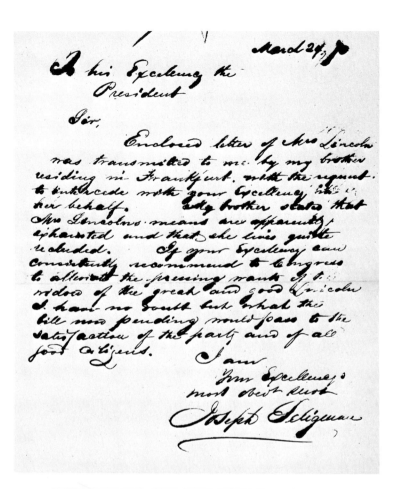

One William Street, the headquarters of the bankers Seligman, was built by them in 1907. Seligman & Company was "one of the strongest and oldest American banking-houses," according to Wall Street authorities of the time. (*Collection of Carl J. White*)

The Grand Union Hotel, Saratoga, New York, where in 1877 Joseph Seligman, America's most prominent Jew, was refused accommodations. The ensuing Hilton-Seligman dispute for the first time drew national attention to the problem of antisemitism in America. The hotel, one of the world's largest, was demolished in 1952. (*Saratoga Historical Society*)

and, allowing himself a half smile, replied soberly, "I agree that you should change your name, William. I suggest you change it to *schlemiel.*"

While other rich German Jews educated their children at the Sachs Collegiate Institute on West Fifty-ninth Street, run by a Teutonic Doktor Sachs, Joseph Seligman, forever the Americanizer, hit on the idea of having Horatio Alger, the creator of American boy heroes, tutor his five sons. Alger, then in his thirties, joined the family and proved to be anything but a red-blooded American boy hero. Short, timid, and very nearsighted, he was easily intimidated by the Seligman sons, who often punished him by locking him in a closet or trunk. But poor Alger, a meek little man, forgave all. In off hours he would practice ballet steps, and at Seligman dinner parties he frequently swooned in social shock. In later life Alger became a rich man, his royalties having been invested by the Seligmans. He died poor, however, having given charity to too many street boys.

In the summer of 1877, when Seligman was fifty-eight and the most prominent Jew in America, there occurred a public act of antisemitism that has come down to us as the Hilton-Seligman affair. At the time there were in the United States about 300,000 Jews, many of whom had already experienced vicious antisemitism. But because of the power of the players in the Hilton-Seligman quarrel, trivial as it was, the problem of antisemitism in America commanded national attention for the first time.

A. T. Stewart of New York, America's greatest retail merchant, had died in 1876, leaving his vast estate in the hands of Judge Henry Hilton, a friend and Stewart's executor. A small-time New York politician and member of the corrupt Tweed Ring, Hilton became important only as he succeeded to the control of the Stewart fortune. One of the many Stewart holdings, then under the control of Judge Hilton, was the Grand Union Hotel in Saratoga.

Saratoga was, at its height, the summer social capital of the American rich. Vulgar, rude, and pretentious, the wealthy flocked to the gambling spa to show off their money, jew-els, and designer clothes in the face of the depression that had followed the Panic of 1873. Foregathered there during the vacation months were bankers, merchant princes, politicians, railroad magnates, society beaux and belles, and the sporting fraternity that made up that so-called Gilded Age. Saratoga had all the sweet taste of a modern Las Vegas. The young Henry James described it as "characteristically American, where riches, finery and possessions ruled." At the center of this dazzling, if somewhat tawdry, elegance stood the imposing Grand Union Hotel.

On June 13, 1877, the banker Joseph Seligman and his family arrived at this queen of Saratoga's hotels, seeking accommodations; he had in the past ten years frequently been a guest there. This time, however, the desk clerk

The Reverend Henry Ward Beecher, the most popular and respected preacher of his day, supported the banker Seligman and attacked the Saratoga antisemites as "men who made their money yesterday, selling codfish." (*J. & W. Seligman & Co.*)

The young and arrogant
August Belmont, born
August Schönberg in
Germany's Rhineland.
(*Library of Congress*)

said to him, "Mr. Seligman, I am required to inform you that Judge Hilton has given instructions that no Israelites shall be permitted in the future to stop at this hotel." Seligman, fighting mad and an avowed enemy of the Tweed Ring and of Judge Hilton, wrote a bitter denunciation of the politician, which he released to the newspapers. It created a national furor. Seligman, the adviser to presidents, a very powerful and well-respected Wall Street banker, had been faced with a NO JEWS WANTED sign. Charges and countercharges, recriminations and name-calling, and threats and counterthreats of legal suits quickly followed. The fraternity of news reporters was having a field

day, and the issue of antisemitism was at front and center stage. Hilton added fuel to the fire by commenting that he would continue his hotel policy "notwithstanding the objections of Moses and all his descendants."

The Reverend Henry Ward Beecher, the most popular and respected preacher of his day, attacked the Saratoga smart set with the words that American "society is so developed that it will not consent to go unless everybody that comes is fit to associate with men who made their money yesterday, selling codfish." In a word to Seligman and his Jewish colleagues the kind minister besought them to be measured in their response to a public insult: "A hero may be annoyed by a mosquito; but to put on his whole armor and call on his followers to join him in making war on an insect would be beneath his dignity." On the other hand, there was Austin Corbin, president of the Long Island Railroad, still the worst commuter line in the nation, who tried to ban Jewish passengers with the statement "We do not like Jews as a class."

By and large Americans supported Seligman in his fight against bigotry, but the incident left ugly scars. In its aftermath indignant Jews and Christians refused to shop at A. T. Stewart stores, thus greatly diminishing the Stewart fortune and ruining Judge Hilton. Three years after the affair Seligman, the banker who stood closest to President Grant, died of a stroke brought on by the acrid dispute. There was no letter of condolence from Judge Hilton.

A Jew of a completely different hue was August Belmont. Seligman, who rose from poor peddler to the lofty status of founder of the House of Seligman, which in 1910 was to put together the General Motors Corporation, climbed the ladder of success the hard way. Belmont, his future assured, came to America as the representative of the House of Rothschild. He never traveled in steerage.

Born in 1816 in Germany's Rhineland, Belmont was the son of Simon Schönberg, a poor merchant. A wild, often violent boy, young Schönberg was harsh and cruel even to his parents, who failed to discipline their unruly son. Yet he had a passionate drive to make money and a razor-sharp mind to back it. At thirteen he ran away from home and in Frankfurt managed to become an apprentice to the Rothschilds, the leading Jewish bankers in Europe. Uneducated and rude, Schönberg shocked the cultivated Rothschilds with his manners but survived in the firm as an acknowledged financial genius. His behavior was so appalling that the Rothschilds transferred him first to Naples and then to Havana, far from Frankfurt. At twenty-one he arrived in New York during the Panic of 1837 and, armed with Rothschild money, began buying stock in a severely depressed market. Somewhere between Havana

and New York, August Schönberg was transformed into August Belmont, the French equivalent of *Schönberg,* meaning "beautiful mountain." In New York he became a self-made man of mystery, a "Frenchman" vaguely connected with the royal families, a banker of enormous wealth and a gentile. Belmont himself was the leading promoter of the legend, which passed muster among New York's belles but not among the Jews. In New York, too, he was able to save failing banks by negotiating huge loans from the House of Rothschild at splendid interest rates. Belmont, almost single-handedly, held the financial center of the nation together following the Panic of 1837. This made him many dependents in the banking community and in the highest echelons of the United States government. Before he was twenty-five Belmont was a major factor in American finance, a situation that was to make the Rothschilds even richer.

An English Rothschild once remarked: "It must be terrible to be a Jew and not be named Rothschild." Belmont must have taken the smug comment to heart, for the young Jewish poseur could not wait to pass into the gentile establishment. Short, stout, and crudely abrasive, he nonetheless fascinated the fatuous ladies of his day with his Continental manners, his wealth, his magnetic eyes, and his languages, which he spoke with an atrocious accent. After all, he was so *masculine;* his hostesses never seemed to notice that they were entertaining a boor. There was little visible antisemitism at the time—this was thirty years before the Hilton-Seligman affair—and Belmont, the society beau, moved freely among the gentile rich. The Jewish upper crust—the Gomezes, the Seixases, the Levys, and the Frankses, among whom were several whose families dated from Peter Stuyvesant's time—largely ignored the parvenu.

Belmont, a first-magnitude social climber, was never to be dismissed with a shrug. In 1841, when the firm of Belmont was an established power on Wall Street, he ordered the invitation committee of the Assembly Ball, the most prestigious social event of its time, to invite him to the ball. With an instinct for the jugular

The middle-aged and still arrogant August Belmont. (*American Jewish Archives, Cincinnati*)

A magazine cartoon mocking the social pretensions of the German Jewish rich. (*American Jewish Archives, Cincinnati*)

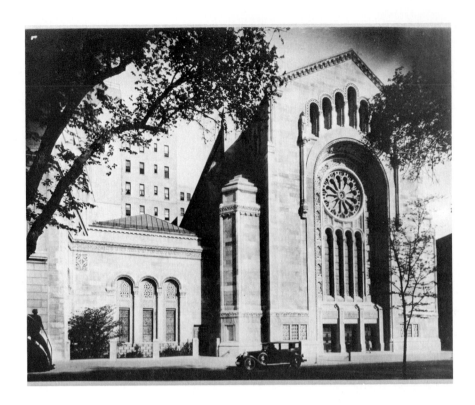

Temple Emanu-El on Fifth Avenue, built by the German Jewish establishment, was designed to look more like a Protestant church than a Jewish synagogue. (*American Jewish Archives, Cincinnati*)

that was never to leave him, Belmont told the members of the assembly that he had investigated "the accounts of you gentlemen on the Street. I can assure you that either I get an invitation to the Assembly this year or else the day after the Assembly each of you will be a ruined man." An invitation was issued, and for the next three or four decades New York society was to dance to the tune of August Belmont, harsh and cheap as it was. But no matter, New York society had for some time been taken to task for its crudeness by many foreign visitors, and even the *New York Herald* complained that "the secret of all this vulgarity in Society is that wealth, or the reputation of wealth, constitutes the open sesame to Society's delectable precincts." Success in America had already become its own justification. Belmont and the gentile rich deserved each other.

In 1848, when Belmont was thirty-two, he married Caroline Slidell Perry, the daughter of Commodore Matthew Perry, the naval officer who later opened Japan to Western trade. Belmont had chosen his young bride as carefully as he chose his wines, his horses, his investments, and his religion. The Perrys were very

social but not rich, and Belmont, by then the banker's banker, needed as much social cachet as he could get. Dreamy, pretty, and impressionable was the creature Caroline, who was wont to weep bitter tears over the miserable poor who lived below Canal Street. The wedding at Grace Church, conducted by an Episcopal clergyman, was the most glittering social event of the season. A few weeks before his nuptials Belmont, as cynical as ever, attained his goal: He was invited to join the Union Club, the most antisemitic club in New York.

Soon after the marriage the young couple established themselves in a mansion on lower Fifth Avenue, near Washington Square. It was the most magnificent residence in New York. Its ballroom, the first of its kind in New York, was designed for the hundreds who attended the annual Belmont ball. His reputation as a host gave his dinner parties, famous for their fine wines and even finer food, a special priority; if invited, a socialite would not dare miss one. It is said that Belmont spent $20,000 a month on wines alone. Two hundred dinner guests would sit down at table and be served by an equal number of footmen on the famous

Belmont gold ware. His many servants wore the Belmont livery: maroon coats, with scarlet piping and silver buttons embossed with the so-called Belmont crest, and black satin knee breeches with silver buckles. The Belmont carriages bore the same colors and crest. At their summer mansion in Newport, Caroline Belmont, ever under the thumb of husband August, struck vacuous poses in regal splendor.

In sheer opulent bad taste few, not even J. P. Morgan, surpassed August Belmont. Before the 1870s the bankers Seligman, Belmont, and Morgan, leading rivals on Wall Street, were doing deals together in private that would make them even richer. Morgan, the head of the triumvirate and its youngest member, would always refer to his colleagues and competitors as the Jews.

Willett Street, on the Lower East Side, in the Gay Nineties. Immigrant Jews flocked to the cheap-rent downtown ghetto in search of the American dream, while their uptown German brethren lived proudly. (*The Children's Aid Society*)

Meyer Guggenheim, seated center, and his seven sons. From left to right: Benjamin, Murry, Isaac, Daniel, Solomon, Simon, and William. At one time the Guggenheims, a worldwide mining dynasty, were as rich and powerful as the Rockefeller brothers. (*Guggenheim Brothers*)

In 1890, at the age of seventy-four, Belmont died and was buried in an ostentatious Christian ceremony. Only in America could a Jewish immigrant, with Rothschild connections, become an August Belmont.

The German Jewish establishment in New York, after Belmont, tended to isolate itself from the gentile wealthy, while still striving toward assimilation. Despite the social contradiction, the peddlers who had become Wall Street powers seemed to thrive in their citadels on upper Fifth Avenue or in their mansions between East Sixtieth and East Eightieth streets, the primest of prime Manhattan real estate. The gentile establishment lived right next door. Germans being a herd species, the One Hun-

dred enjoyed their own special status as a society within a society. Their dinner parties, galas, and vacation retreats were limited to their own kind and even department store magnates such as the Gimbels were excluded. After all, they were just shopkeepers. One can only imagine their social embarrassment with the myriad of wretched Jews trying to survive on the Lower East Side. Their answer to the squalid conditions of the tenement poor—sickness, housing, jobs, and despair—was the settlement house, which was to serve ghetto Jews as an inspiration for social betterment, by writ of the One Hundred.

Among the Seligmans, Loebs, Sachses, Guggenheims, Schiffs, Warburgs, Lewisohns,

Daniel Guggenheim, the most astute of the brothers, who beat the Rockefellers at their own game. (*Guggenheim Brothers*)

Kahns, Kuhns, Goldmans, Goodharts, Lehmans, Baches, Altschuls, and many other Wall Street families, intermarriage was commonplace. To marry outside the establishment would have set a dangerous trend. So imbued had the One Hundred become with the values of the Four Hundred, their social superiors, that their temple, Emanu-El, on Fifth Avenue was designed to look more like a Protestant church than a Jewish synagogue. This was a high point in the history of Jewish assimilation in America.

In 1894, in an article published by the *Yiddishe Gazette,* a Lower East Side immigrant wrote feelingly about rich uptown Jews: "We do not want to criticize our German brethren. We have our faults too—It is up to us, the Russian Jews, to help our poor countrymen and keep them from being insulted by our proud brethren to whom a Russian Jew is a *schnorrer,* a tramp, a good-for-nothing. . . . In the philanthropic institutions of our aristocratic German Jews you see magnificent offices, with lavish desks, but along with this, morose and angry faces. A poor man is questioned like a criminal. He trembles like a leaf, as if he were standing before a Russian official."

Simon Guggenheim, the patriarch of the Guggenheim dynasty, which at one time controlled as much wealth in America as the Rockefellers, was born a ghetto Jew, a tailor, in Switzerland. In 1848 the fifty-six-year-old Simon and his twelve children arrived in Philadelphia, after a two-month voyage in steerage. Like the Seligmans before them, Simon and his eldest son, Meyer, took to foot peddling in the dreary backcountry of Pennsylvania. Meyer, then twenty, was to become the founder of the Guggenheim fortune.

Father and son endured incredible hardships in the coal-mining towns of Pennsylvania, peddling their needles and pins, ribbons, shoelaces, and sundries, until Meyer Guggenheim, good-looking and very bright, struck on the idea of a new kind of stove polish. Iron stoves had to be cleaned, but the housewives along his route complained that the existing polish burned their hands and stained their clothes. With his usual business acumen, the young man developed a noncaustic stove polish that became an instant success. The father, by then too old to bear the rigors of peddling, was placed in charge of the vats brewing the stove polish, while the son continued to peddle the polish in the coal country. Meyer soon added Guggenheim's blueing and Guggenheim's lye to his household line.

Within a few years Meyer Guggenheim sold his stove polish and lye company for $150,000 and branched out in other directions—herbs and spices from the West Indies and lace and embroidery from Switzerland. He also speculated in the stock market, where, in one deal alone, the Hannibal & St. Joseph Railroad, he made half a million dollars. His fortune grew, as did his family: He and his wife, Barbara, had seven sons: Isaac, Daniel, Murry, Solomon, Benjamin, Simon, and William. They were to become known as the Guggenheim Brothers, an enormously rich and powerful clan of American capitalists, not unlike the Rockefeller Brothers.

The pivotal event in Meyer Guggenheim's financial career took place after the Civil War, when Charles Graham, a Philadelphia Quaker, applied to him for a loan. Graham owned some silver and lead mining properties in Leadville, Colorado, that needed exploitation. He was so enthusiastic that he succeeded in selling Guggenheim a partnership. Silver and lead were indeed discovered in the Graham mines, after months of travail and forbidding expenses, and

Meyer Guggenheim became a multimillionaire. From that time on, the West Indian spice trade and the Swiss embroidery business, although profitable, were virtually forgotten. Guggenheim jumped into mining and smelting with both feet. By 1882 his mining holdings were so extensive that he formed M. Guggenheim's Sons, in which each of his seven sons was an equal partner; Daniel was more equal than the others since he was the most astute. Well trained and knowledgeable, the sons bought their first smelter in 1888 in Pueblo, Colorado, for half a million and soon after acquired another in Mexico. One of their mine holdings in 1890 was worth more than $14 million.

In 1889 Guggenheim, then more than sixty, and his tribe pulled up stakes in Philadelphia and moved to New York, the financial center of the United States. From their paneled boardroom in lower Manhattan, Meyer and his boys built a worldwide mining empire that stretched from the Yukon in the north to Mexico, Bolivia, and Chile in the south and from there to Angola and the Congo in Africa. Silver, gold, copper, zinc, lead, nitrates, and other profitable metals and minerals were extracted from distant mines and refined in Guggenheim smelters. The family founded the Colorado Smelting and Refining Company, Kennecott Copper Corporation, Nevada Consolidated, the Esperanza Gold Mine in Mexico, and the Chile Copper Company, among other gigantic operations. In some years Guggenheim enterprises produced more than one-half of the world's copper supply.

In 1898 Adolph Lewisohn and his brother, Jewish mining entrepreneurs, as were the Guggenheims, decided to join forces with the Rockefellers of Standard Oil and Anaconda Copper in an ambitious scheme to take over control of metals production in the United States. Their joint venture, called the American Smelting and Refining Company, represented a merger of twenty-three smelting firms. The Guggenheims, deeply suspicious of any plan that would put copper production into the hands of the Lewisohns and Rockefellers, politely declined an invitation to join the trust. Led by the brilliant Daniel Guggenheim, and after consultations with old Meyer, the broth-

ers chose to fight. First they dumped lead on the market at below cost, thus forcing losses on the trust. Then they took advantage of a miners' strike against the trust to depress further the price of American Smelting and Refining stock, and when the shares hit bottom, the Guggenheims quietly bought up huge blocs of stock in the company. When the smoke finally cleared, Daniel Guggenheim was president of American Smelting and Refining and four of his brothers were on the board of directors. AS&R was a Guggenheim firm.

Meyer Guggenheim, the king of Copper, died in 1905 at the age of seventy-six. He had come a very long way from his days of peddling stove polish in the anthracite country. His sharp-witted son Daniel inherited the royal title and scepter.

Henry Lehman, the first of the Lehman brothers to arrive in the United States from Bavaria, became a peddler in Alabama. By 1845 he was settled in Montgomery, then a muddy, rat-infested, and fever-ridden town with high hopes of becoming a cotton capital. Linked to Mobile and New Orleans by the Alabama River, the town prospered in the cotton trade. Henry led a lonely and celibate life, living in a room behind his shop so that he could save money to send for his brothers, Emanuel and Mayer, still in Bavaria. Within five years his frugality was rewarded, and Emanuel and Mayer joined Henry as cotton brokers in Montgomery. The firm of Lehman Brothers, which was to become a banking force on Wall Street, was born.

With a thriving cotton business in Montgomery, the Lehmans acquired the style of Southern gentlemen: They owned slaves, spoke with deep Southern accents, and enjoyed an appetite for Southern cooking. More and more money was flowing in from New York, then the true center of the cotton economy, and Emanuel Lehman was frequently dispatched to Manhattan to watch over Lehman interests. In 1855 Henry, then only thirty-three and the oldest brother, died in a yellow fever epidemic. Emanuel, twenty-nine, and Mayer, twenty-six, were left to carry on.

Within a few years the two remaining Lehman brothers felt it necessary to establish a permanent office in New York, and Emanuel, already experienced in Wall Street finance, set up shop on Liberty Street, not far from the Seligmans, a family he deeply admired. In 1858 he married Pauline Sondheim, a Jewish girl from New York, and they rented a brownstone in fashionable Murray Hill, again not far from the Seligmans. Mayer Lehman, meanwhile, remained in Montgomery, running the cotton business that provided the revenues for the New York operation. He married Babette Newgass, a New Orleans girl, who was related to

Bernard Baruch, a financial wizard and the economic adviser to heads of state, discussing life with Harry F. Guggenheim, soldier, diplomat, and mining executive, at Saratoga Racetrack. Harry was the son of the great Daniel Guggenheim. (*Guggenheim Brothers*)

the rich Hellmans of San Francisco, who in turn were related to the Seligmans of New York. It was a prudent marriage.

The Union blockage of Southern cotton shipments to the North during the Civil War severely damaged Emanuel Lehman's financial position in New York. Mayer, a staunch supporter of the Confederacy, was hailed as "one of the best Southern patriots." He was to name his youngest son, Herbert H. Lehman, who became a national political figure in the twentieth century, after Hilary A. Herbert, a well-known Confederate political leader. In the North, Emanuel, a Southerner by sympathy, undertook the selling of Confederate bonds in Eu-

rope, with some success. His chief competitor in London was Joseph Seligman, who as Lincoln's agent was promoting the sale of Union securities.

After the war the Lehmans quickly restored their cotton business, and in 1868 Mayer Lehman left Montgomery to join his brother in New York, where in new offices in Pearl Street Lehman Brothers could profit from fluctuations in the cotton market. The business in the South was placed in the hands of trusted partners and relatives. On New York's Cotton Exchange the Lehmans soon became a major factor, one to be reckoned with, in the speculative buying and selling of cotton. Emanuel, conservative and cautious, and Mayer, bold and outgoing, were opposites in temperament, but none questioned their business acumen.

By the 1890s the firm of Lehman Brothers—by then a large commodities house dealing in cotton, coffee, and petroleum—had five Lehmans: Mayer and Emanuel, their respective sons Sigmund and Philip, and Meyer H. Lehman, the son of Henry, the Lehman brother who had died in the South some years before.

Mayer Lehman, from cotton broker in Montgomery, Alabama, to Wall Street financier. One of the original Lehman Brothers, he was the father of Herbert H. Lehman. (*American Jewish Archives, Cincinnati*)

Herbert H. Lehman, governor and senator and one of America's most distinguished statesmen. (*American Jewish Archives, Cincinnati*)

Wall Street, the scene of many financial battles and wars, in 1903. In the background is Trinity Church, the seat of America's richest parish; colonial Jews had contributed to the building of the original steeple in 1711. (*J. & W. Seligman & Co.*)

While the Lehmans were a success in the financial district, in those early days they were ranked far below the Kuhn, Loebs, for example, to say nothing of the Seligmans, Schiffs, Warburgs, and Guggenheims. Often stodgy, the family had at least one free spirit, Herbert H. Lehman. When young Herbert entered Williams College in 1895, he arrived on campus in his own car, a rarity then, driven by his own chauffeur, an even rarer sight.

After Mayer and Emanuel died, the Lehman cousins, led by the hard-driving Philip, took control of the business. Eager and ambitious, the Lehman boys became private investment bankers, backing new and risky enter-

prises that would make them a fortune. Lehman Brothers together with Goldman, Sachs, firms that were connected by friendship and matrimonial ties, had by 1914 underwritten such budding companies as Sears, Roebuck, Underwood, Studebaker, F. W. Woolworth, and Continental Can. In the 1930s Lehman and Goldman, Sachs parted company after several acrimonious disputes, and each went its own way to greater glory and riches.

In later times Robert Lehman replaced his father, Philip, as head of the firm; Robert, before he died, had become a world-renowned art collector. Today, following a merger with Kuhn, Loeb, the firm of Lehman Brothers Kuhn

Loeb Inc. is one of the most powerful financial forces on Wall Street.

In 1849 Solomon Loeb, a sickly and neurotic twenty-year-old from the Rhineland, arrived in America via steerage. The son of a poor Jewish merchant, he had been sent to his cousins the Kuhns in Cincinnati, where, it was hoped, he could escape the poverty and anti-semitism of Germany. His parents' dreams were to be realized far beyond all expectation.

Cincinnati, at the time the third or fourth largest city in the United States, was an active river port and a meat-packing center, nick-named Porkopolis. Young Loeb took to his newly adopted city happily, if that word can be used to describe the feelings of a hypochondriac, and joined his cousin Abraham Kuhn in the dry goods business. It became quickly apparent that Loeb was a born salesman who understood the value of money. Abe Kuhn had started a small clothing factory, and when business was looking good in Cincinnati, he decided to open an outlet in downtown Manhattan with Sol Loeb in charge. Thus, Kuhn, Loeb & Com-

Jacob Henry Schiff, seated behind and slightly to the right of his friend, the then vice president, Theodore Roosevelt, in 1900. The occasion marked the groundbreaking ceremonies for Montefiore Hospital in New York. (*Montefiore Hospital and Medical Center, the Bronx*)

Jacob Henry Schiff, one of Wall Street's most brilliant financiers, who ran his business and his family in *ein, zwei, drei* fashion. (*UPI*)

pany, clothing manufacturers, was born. As the firm prospered, more and more Kuhns and Loebs—thirteen in all—arrived in Cincinnati from Germany and went to work for the factory. So intermarried and clannish did the two families become that they were known simply as the Kuhn, Loebs.

By 1870 the firm of Kuhn, Loeb was well established on Wall Street, not as clothing manufacturers or dry goods merchants but as investment bankers, so well had Solomon Loeb done. His partner Abe Kuhn, by then a millionaire, had left the business and returned to the fatherland in search of *Kultur* and *Gemütlichkeit.* Solomon and his wife, Betty, who detested Cincinnati, were comfortably settled in a brownstone in the Murray Hill district, not too far from the Seligmans.

While in Germany, Kuhn, the ultimate German Jewish romantic, discovered Jacob Henry Schiff, a young, cold-eyed Jewish banker in Frankfurt, who was considerably less than romantic. In 1874, when Schiff was twenty-seven years old, Kuhn invited him to join Kuhn, Loeb & Company in New York. This was to be Abe Kuhn's greatest and most lasting contribution to the firm. A year after arriving in New York, the handsome Jacob Schiff married the sweet but plain Therese Loeb, the daughter of Solomon Loeb. It was a marriage made in the boardroom with little help from heaven.

Jacob Henry, the son of Moses and Clara Schiff, could trace his Teutonic lineage back to 1370. His family tree, according to him, was adorned with Jewish scholars of distinction and superior men of affairs. Schiff himself attended local schools in Frankfurt, and at fourteen he was apprenticed to a business firm. In 1885, at the age of thirty-eight, Schiff became head of Kuhn, Loeb. His cool intelligence and penetrating mind were to raise the firm from the ranks of the third-rate to top-of-the-line Wall Street bankers. A martinet, he ran his office and his family in *eins, zwei, drei* fashion.

In America, Schiff became very interested in the railroad-building boom. In short order he involved Kuhn, Loeb in railroad financing and reorganization, which were to bring tremendous profits to the firm. The Pennsylvania Railroad, the Louisville & Nashville, and the Baltimore & Ohio were among the railways influenced by Schiff. Probably the most sensational episode in his financial career was the struggle of Schiff, who had allied himself with the Harrimans, against the House of Morgan for control of the Union Pacific and Northern Pacific railroads. So vigorous was the battle that it brought about a small Wall Street panic in 1901.

Schiff, a brilliant financier, at various times came to the aid of American Smelting & Refining, Westinghouse Electric, and Western Union Telegraph. His financial dimensions were enormous; in 1904, at the start of the Russo-Japanese War, he secured a $200 million loan for Japan.

In philanthropy the name of Jacob Henry Schiff was legend. Unlike the great Judah Touro, however, Schiff was swayed by moral edification rather than by humanitarian impulses. He helped promote Tuskegee Institute and other black schools in the South and was a benefactor of the Henry Street Settlement on the Lower East Side, although he had little regard for ghetto Jews. He aided Columbia, Harvard, Barnard, Cornell, and other academic institutions, while making major contributions to the Jewish Theological Seminary of New York and Hebrew Union College in Cincinnati. Montefiore Hospital in New York was virtually built by Jacob Henry Schiff.

Deeply religious, the impeccable Schiff expressed his special obligation to the Jewish people when he declined to participate in an international loan to Russia because he resented the czar's antisemitic treatment of Jews. Yet he remained an enigma to the Russian Jewish immigrants who were flooding the Lower East Side; the great banker, the international mover and shaker, made them feel like *schnorrers.* Schiff, a good man but a better German, seemed to lack the human touch.

Frieda Schiff, the daughter of Jacob Schiff and Therese Loeb, was a lovely, dewy-eyed maiden, completely dominated by her father. In 1894, while on the annual Schiff family tour of Germany, young Frieda met and captivated the handsome Felix M. Warburg, one of Germany's most eligible Jewish bachelors. "I don't *think* I flirted," she said years later, "because I had been brought up so strictly, and had gone out so little, that I was not too certain of myself." Of course, Jacob Schiff, the leading partner of Kuhn, Loeb & Company, and Moritz Warburg, the head of the House of Warburg in Hamburg, had certain marriage arrangements to conclude. Frieda and Felix were married in 1895, and two years later Warburg became a partner in his father-in-law's banking firm in New York. Frieda, on the other hand, had been born a Loeb and a Schiff and was now a Warburg; she had become the link connecting three major fortunes.

The House of Warburg, an international banking firm, had been founded in Hamburg in 1798 by Felix's great-grandfather. The Warburg family was said to have originated centuries before in Italy and claimed to be one of the world's most aristocratic Jewish families. Felix, a *bon vivant* in Germany, the lover of beautiful women, music, art, books, clothes, and yachts, settled with Frieda in New York and became a fine family man.

Their opulent mansion at the corner of Ninety-second Street and Fifth Avenue remains a Manhattan landmark. Warburg, as it turned out, was much more interested in philanthropy than in banking, and with Frieda at his side, the former man-about-town gained a well-deserved reputation as a humanist. Among the charities to which he lent his financial support and leadership were the Juilliard School of Music (Warburg had once played the violin), the New York Symphony Society, the Fogg Art Museum at Harvard, the American Foundation for the Blind, Teachers College at Columbia, the Educational Alliance, the Henry Street Settlement, the Jewish Board of Guardians, which provided psychiatric care for disturbed children, the Federation of Jewish Philanthropies, the Jewish Theological Seminary, and many hospitals and other philanthropies. A kindly man, Warburg believed in human betterment through culture and education, to which he gave much time, energy, and wealth.

Otto Hermann Kahn, known to history as the Jewish Medici, was born in Mannheim,

Jewish Theological Seminary in New York City, the house that Jacob Schiff built. It was among his many philanthropies. (*American Jewish Archives, Cincinnati*)

Germany, in 1867, the son of a reputable banking family. He was reared in an atmosphere of culture and art and learned to play the violin and the cello at an early age. At seventeen he had already written two five-act tragedies in blank verse, which were never to be performed, for obvious reasons. Educated at home and at the University of Karlsruhe, Kahn was inducted into the German hussars at twenty and served his regiment with pride and distinction. His erect, soldierly bearing was to become his social hallmark in New York.

In 1888 he joined the Deutsche Bank in Berlin and was sent to its London branch. Kahn spent five years in England, where he became a committed Anglophile. His reputation as a brilliant, young banker was noted by "the

Frieda Schiff Warburg, the granddaughter of Solomon Loeb, the daughter of Jacob Henry Schiff, and the wife of Felix M. Warburg, was the link connecting three large fortunes. She was a gracious lady of many philanthropies. (*American Jewish Archives, Cincinnati*)

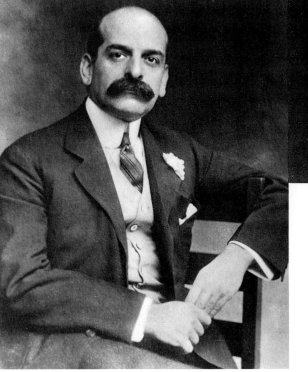

The handsome Felix M. Warburg, a warmhearted banker and philanthropist, son-in-law to Jacob Henry Schiff. A *bon vivant* as a youth, Felix became a fine family man. (*American Jewish Archives, Cincinnati*)

Felix and Frieda Warburg lived comfortably in their opulent mansion on the corner of Ninety-second Street and Fifth Avenue, still a Manhattan landmark. The photograph was taken in 1935 at the nadir of the Depression. (*Wide World Photos*)

Otto Hermann Kahn, the banker-impresario, who brought the
golden age of opera to America, in 1930. The wealthy Kahn was
known as the Jewish Medici. (*Wide World Photos*)

crowd" on Wall Street, and in 1893 he accepted a position with the banking house of Speyer & Company in New York. This was to be of short tenure since Kahn really preferred art and music and the good life to office humdrum. While in New York, he met and then married Addie Wolff, the wealthy daughter of Abraham Wolff, a partner at Kuhn, Loeb & Company. A year later the thirty-year-old banker became a member of the firm.

Jacob Henry Schiff, a fine judge of rising young bankers, took a fancy to the young Kahn despite his excursions into the frivolous world of art and music. Edward H. Harriman, the railroad tycoon, became Kahn's close friend and depended upon him for much of the financing of his titanic railroad transactions, with Schiff's approval. As it turned out, Kahn proved to be a financial genius and a valuable aide to Harriman in reorganizing the Union Pacific, Baltimore & Ohio, Missouri Pacific, Wabash, Texas & Pacific, and Denver & Rio Grande railroads. These deeds often shook Wall Street but brought great wealth to Kuhn, Loeb and to the former hussar, Otto Hermann Kahn.

Kahn became interested in the Metropolitan Opera in 1903, and in 1907 he and William K. Vanderbilt decided to buy the faltering company. A new Metropolitan Opera Company was organized, and soon after that the Jew with the princely manner bought out the Vanderbilts. It was Otto Kahn, the owner of the Metropolitan, who brought the golden age of opera to America and the Met to international recognition when he acquired Giulio Gatti-Casazza, the director of La Scala at Milan, Arturo Toscanini, and Enrico Caruso for his gilded opera house.

The banker-impresario also put together a superb collection of Old Master paintings, which further enhanced his reputation as America's leading art patron. The full extent of his generosities to the arts will never be known since he concealed many of his gifts; in 1930 it was discovered that he had for years been giving money prizes to black artists in New York and had advanced a large sum toward the restoration of the Parthenon in Athens. His stately manor in England and his homes on Fifth Avenue in Manhattan and at Cold Spring Harbor, Long Island, were international showplaces, noted for their luxury, their style, and their wealth of furnishings.

His contributions to art and culture having been noticed by the press, Otto Hermann Kahn, in many ways a secret sharer, was approached

One of Otto Kahn's princely manors, his magnificent estate at Cold Spring Harbor, Long Island. Only an aerial view, taken in the 1930s, could encompass the extent of his domain. (*Wide World Photos*)

An early nineteenth-century daguerreotype of the Straus home in Otterberg, Germany. The family came a long way from Otterberg. (*Nathan Straus III*)

by a callow reporter for an explanation. "I must atone for my wealth," the banker dryly replied.

The illustrious Straus family of New York originated in the village of Otterberg, Bavaria, in early times. Lazarus Straus, the patriarch, fleeing a German political upheaval and a new surge of antisemitism in the fatherland, emigrated to America in 1852, and he and his large family settled in Talbotton, Georgia, a Southern town in the middle of nowhere. There Straus and his two oldest sons, Isidor and Nathan, both having been educated in log cabin schools, established themselves as a reputable and successful merchant family.

During the Civil War, Isidor went to Europe to purchase supplies for the Confederacy and to sell Confederate bonds. After the devastation of the war, however, the senior Straus decided to move the family to New York City, where the Strauses were to become prominent as merchants, philanthropists, and public servants. In 1866 the importing firm of L. Straus and Sons was formed in Manhattan. Years of struggle brought Isidor and his brother Nathan into a partnership with the well-known merchant Rowland H. Macy; in 1896 the brothers acquired sole ownership of R. H. Macy and Company and developed it into the biggest department store in the world. They also built up the Brooklyn department store of Abraham & Straus.

The brothers complemented each other superbly. Isidor's financial and merchandising acumen were supported by Nathan's creative and more enterprising nature. They engineered the risky move of Macy's from Fourteenth Street uptown to Herald Square. It proved wildly profitable and transported Macy's solidly into the twentieth century.

In 1912 tragedy struck the family. Isidor Straus and his wife, the former Ida Blun, went down with the *Titanic* on its ill-fated maiden voyage across the Atlantic. When the order was given for women and children to take to the lifeboats, Ida, a strong and sweet lady, refused to leave her husband of forty years, while Isidor declined a place on the boats so long as any women remained on board.

Nathan Straus, sensitive and compassionate as a boy, became a bold humanitarian as a man. The department store tycoon distributed food and buckets of coal to the freezing poor during the 1890s; in the winter of '92 he gave away 1.5 million buckets of coal to the unemployed. Subsequent winters produced more homeless and needy, and "Nathan the Kind" responded by establishing lodging houses, where bed and breakfast were provided for five cents. In 1894 Straus, a very popular figure in New York, was offered the Democratic nomination for mayor but declined the honor.

During the Gay Nineties, as history has labeled that dressy but impoverished period, Nathan Straus became deeply concerned with the number of children dying of tainted milk; in 1891, 241 of every 1,000 infants born in New York City died before their first birthdays largely because of diseased milk. Straus and his wife, Lina, launched a campaign for the pasteurization of milk, during which they had to combat public ignorance, commercial greed, and political indifference. Their strenuous efforts led ultimately to the compulsory pasteurization of milk in most American cities; by 1909 the death rate among children had been halved. Nathan Straus opened pasteurized-milk stations in more than thirty cities in the United States at his own expense. Layman though he was, Straus lives in the annals of medicine as a pioneer in public health.

From his early years, Straus, an ardent Zionist, was devoted to Palestine, and in the last decade of his life he gave nearly two-thirds of his fortune to Jewish causes in Palestine.

Isidor Straus and his brother Nathan developed Macy's department store into the world's largest. A businessman of rare acumen, Isidor went down with the ill-fated *Titanic* in 1912. (*Macy's*)

Nathan Straus in later times, compassionate humanitarian and friend to the poor. As a result of his efforts, pasteurization of milk for children was introduced into American cities, thus halving the infant death rate. (*Macy's*)

A daguerreotype of young Nathan Straus taken in Georgia in the 1850s. Nathan, the future department store tycoon, refused to pose unless he could hold his mongrel pup. (*Nathan Straus III*)

He established, among many other health and welfare services, the monumental Nathan and Lina Straus Health Centers in Jerusalem and Tel Aviv. At the entrance to his health center in Jerusalem is an inscription in English, Arabic, and Hebrew proclaiming that the medical facilities are for all inhabitants of the land—Christian, Moslem, and Jew. In 1927, when he was almost eighty, Nathan Straus himself laid the cornerstone.

President William Howard Taft summed up the American judgment when he said, "Dear old Nathan Straus is a great Jew and the greatest Christian of us all."

Oscar Solomon Straus, the youngest of the Straus brothers, was only three when his family settled in Talbotton, Georgia. In New York young Oscar attended prep schools and then Columbia College; he received his law degree in 1873. Oscar Straus, unlike his brothers, never had the rustic advantages of a log cabin education.

For a while he practiced as a lawyer, and then he joined his brothers in business. It is as a diplomat and public servant, however, that Oscar Straus left his mark on American history. A reform Democrat in politics, he came to the attention of Henry Ward Beecher, the famous Protestant clergyman, who recommended him to President Grover Cleveland; the Reverend Mr. Beecher had become impressed with the tact, energy, and intelligence of Oscar Solomon Straus. In 1887 President Cleveland appointed Straus ambassador to Turkey, his selection being intended by Cleveland as a rebuke to the Austro-Hungary Empire, which had earlier refused to receive an American ambassador because his wife was Jewish. Straus performed his duties so well in Constantinople that in 1890, 1898, and 1909, when affairs in the Ottoman Empire were in a critical state, three successive presidents—McKinley, Roosevelt, and Taft—drafted him for ambassadorial missions. In 1902 he was appointed a member of the Permanent Court of Arbitration at The Hague, and in 1906 Theodore Roosevelt named him secretary of commerce and labor in his cabinet. Oscar Straus had become the most prominent American Jew of his time.

In 1912 he was the Progressive party's nominee for governor of New York, and while the party went down to defeat at the polls, his own popularity was so great that he ran ahead not only of his ticket but even of Theodore Roosevelt himself, the presidential candidate. Straus was an eloquent and persuasive speaker, when animated by his enthusiasms, and a polished writer with many published books, including *Roger Williams: The Pioneer of Religious Liberty* (1894), *The American Spirit* (1913), and his memoirs, *Under Four Administrations: From Cleveland to Taft* (1922). This dynamo of charming energy somehow found the time to marry Sarah Lavanburg in 1882 and bring up a family.

As a Jew by birth and tradition Oscar Straus employed his power and influence to ameliorate the conditions of his coreligionists abroad. In 1903, when the Kishinev pogroms outraged the civilized world, he met first with President Roosevelt to frame a strong protest to the czar and then with Count Sergius Witte, the czar's minister, to discuss the question of antisemitism in Russia. While ambassador to Constantinople he conferred with the sultan on the status of Palestine, then part of the Ottoman Empire, and with Theodor Herzl, the founder of the Zionist movement. At the peace conference after the First World War, Straus was deeply concerned with the safeguarding of the Jewish minorities in Europe. His concern unfortunately was to prove well founded. When he died in 1926, Oscar Solomon Straus was publicly mourned as an outstanding American citizen.

JULIUS OCHS, the founder of a publishing dynasty, was born in Bavaria and emigrated to America in 1845. A cultured youth, he engaged in teaching and in business with little success. His wanderings led him to Kentucky and then to Tennessee, and finally to Nashville. There he met and married the brilliant and forceful Bertha Levy, another Bavarian immigrant; both had come from well-connected German Jewish families. Julius was then twenty-nine.

Their first surviving son, Adolph Simon Ochs, was born in 1858; he was destined to

Oscar Solomon Straus, the youngest of the Straus brothers and the most well-known American Jew of his time. Diplomat and cabinet official, he served under four presidential administrations, beginning with that of Grover Cleveland. In this photograph Oscar and his wife, Sarah, are in mourning for brother Isidor, who died tragically in 1912. (*Library of Congress*)

From left to right, Henry Morgenthau, the man who owned major sections of the Bronx, an unidentified young lady, and Adolph Simon Ochs, the founder of *The New York Times,* having fun on a hobbyhorse in 1927. Ochs, one of the world's greatest newspaper publishers, was a genuine Horatio Alger hero. Morgenthau, a real estate speculator, banker, and diplomat, was the father of Henry Morgenthau, Jr., secretary of the treasury under Franklin D. Roosevelt. (*The Little Art Shop, Glendale, California*)

become the publisher of *The New York Times.* Julius Ochs, despite his long Southern residence and his wife's Southern sympathies, joined the Union army during the Civil War. After the war, as the better part of valor, he moved his family to Knoxville. There Ochs was a communal leader and, for many years, a volunteer rabbi to the Jewish community. So poor had the Ochs family become that young Adolph had to find work at the age of eleven. In later years Adolph Ochs, by then one of America's greatest newspaper publishers, would say that "the printing office was my high school and university." He could have added that his parents, Julius and Bertha, were reasonable substitutes for a more formal education.

Adolph Ochs's first job was as an office boy on the *Knoxville Chronicle,* where he fell in love with the excitement of the newspaper business; soon after that he became a printer's devil in the composing room and learned publishing from the ground up. By the age of nineteen, when he moved to Chattanooga, Adolph Ochs knew newspaper production. When he discovered that the *Chattanooga Times* was on the edge of failure, he took control of the decrepit newspaper for $250. Adolph Ochs had begun his career as a publisher before he was old enough to vote.

Within a few years Ochs, a young man of courage and vision, had turned the *Times* into a profit maker and one of the South's leading papers. In 1883, when he was twenty-five, the promising publisher married Effie Miriam Wise of Cincinnati, daughter of Isaac Mayer Wise, the great leader of Reform Judaism in America. Some years later Iphigene Bertha was born to Adolph and Effie; Iphigene Bertha Ochs was to become *The New York Times* heiress, a charming and astute woman, and the wife of the handsome Arthur Hays Sulzberger, whom she married in 1917. Meanwhile, in Chattanooga, as the town grew so did the newspaper. The Ochs family house became the center of Southern hospitality, and Adolph and Effie entertained many eminent visitors, prominent people who were to be valuable in New York.

In 1896 Ochs heard that *The New York Times,* once prosperous and powerful, was foundering on the verge of bankruptcy; its daily circulation was down to a paltry 9,000, and the paper was losing $1,000 a day. The *World* and the *Journal,* with immense circulations, seemed to have cornered the market in New York with their features on sex, crime, and scandal; it was the era of yellow journalism, which has endured and prospers to the present day. Adolph Ochs, flying in the face of a storm, decided to invest $75,000, largely borrowed from friends, in the moribund *New York Times;* in late 1896, at the age of thirty-six, Ochs, the pride of Chattanooga, became the publisher of *The New York Times.*

A man of principle, he insisted that *The Times* be "clean, dignified, and trustworthy" and invented the slogan "All the News That's Fit to Print." He shunned sensationalism of any kind, while promoting the accuracy of news stories. So pervasive was his moral influence that, it is said, a city editor assigned a story to a reporter with the words "Here's an incest story. Keep it clean."

Loyal to his employees, accessible, and kind, he earned the respect and affection of his staff. Before he died in 1935, after thirty-nine years of publishing *The Times,* he saw its daily circulation rise to almost 500,000. His appeal to the intelligent reader had worked, and *The Times* had become one of the world's greatest newspapers.

The life of Adolph Simon Ochs was rare in that he was a genuine Horatio Alger hero.

THE GERMAN JEWISH establishment held sway for many decades in New York. Mimicking the style of the older gentile establishment, German Jews sought money and power, respectability and the glory of philanthropy, and they were successful. However, they suffered neither fools nor East European immigrants gladly. The social wheel grinds slowly.

In 1852 a son was born to Samuel and Rosalie Michelson in Strelno, Poland, then under German rule. When the boy was little more than a babe in arms, his Polish Jewish parents fled from German persecution and crossed the Atlantic to New York City. There his father worked for a time as a jeweler, unknown and surely unheralded. A venturesome immigrant, Samuel moved his family to Virginia City, Nevada, where he established a dry goods store. His son, Albert Abraham Michelson, was trained at public schools in Nevada and with relatives in San Francisco. According to his teachers, the student Albert was "zealous, loyal, studious, and uncommonly bright." Their reports showed uncommon insight, for Albert Abraham Michelson became the first American scientist to win a Nobel Prize.

Michelson, who was determined to have a college education despite the penurious condition of the family treasury, took the competitive examination to the United States Naval Academy. Although he scored extremely high marks, he did not receive an appointment. So frustrated was he that he decided to discuss his plight with President U. S. Grant; Grant, of course, had never heard of Albert Michelson. At sixteen the youth, sometimes on foot, other times by horse or stagecoach, and finally by rail, traveled the 2,000 miles from Virginia City to the nation's capital. In Washington he learned that it was President Grant's habit to walk his dog in the morning on or near the White House grounds. For days the future Nobel laureate sat on the curb outside the White House, hoping to catch the president's eye. When he did, Grant was so impressed with the young man's story that he gave the determined student a presidential appointment to the Naval Academy. The Civil War hero, the academy, and the American people were to be very proud of that appointment.

As a midshipman at Annapolis, Michelson was outstanding. He was a whiz at science, finishing first in his class in optics, acoustics, and design and second in mathematics. A violinist and artist, the midshipman from Nevada was also a top fencer and tennis player and the academy's lightweight boxing champion. However, he was dismal as a seaman; he finished twenty-fifth in a class of twenty-nine. After he had served a two-year tour of sea duty, the navy thought it wise to recall Michelson to the academy as an instructor.

At Annapolis the young naval officer went to work on a fundamental scientific problem

Iphigene Ochs Sulzberger, daughter of *The Times'* publisher and one of the most gracious ladies of her time. (*The New York Times*)

The handsome Arthur Hays Sulzberger, husband to Iphigene Ochs and publisher of the newspaper after Ochs's death. (*The New York Times*)

Midshipman Albert Abraham Michelson, a member of the class of 1873 at Annapolis. Michelson was the first American scientist to win a Nobel Prize. (*U.S. Naval Academy*)

he had encountered in his early studies in physics: the measurement of the exact speed of light. With the cooperation of the navy, plus a few dollars, Michelson created a simple device of great sensitivity for his experiments. After a year of tests he concluded that the velocity of light in air was 186,508 miles per second. His inexpensive machine, consisting of a lamp, a condensing lens, and a fixed mirror, with another rotating on a vertical spindle, had given science a physical constant and a classic landmark in experimentation. In 1879 he announced his discovery to a distinguished body of scientists and received international recognition in return. Michelson had become an American scientist of stature; he was then twenty-six.

A few years later he resigned from the navy and became a professor of physics at various institutions until he settled at the University of Chicago, where he headed the physics department for thirty-seven years. This modest man, who knew nothing of wealth and power or of social establishments, was awarded the Nobel Prize in physics in 1907.

In 1931 Albert Einstein, on a visit to America, paid tribute to the grand old man of American science at a learned congress. "You, my honored Dr. Michelson," the father of the nuclear age said, "began your work when I was hardly a youngster. It was you who led the physicists into new paths, and through your marvelous experimental work paved the way for the development of the theory of relativity. Without your work this theory would be scarcely more than an interesting speculation."

The ultramodern science building at the Naval Academy, Michelson Hall, was named for one of its most distinguished graduates, the American Jew who taught the world how to measure light, space, and time.

Albert Michelson, the grand old man of American science, and
Albert Einstein, the father of the nuclear age, at a scientific
congress in California in 1931. Michelson, an American Jew, and
Einstein, a German-Swiss Jew, radically changed our
understanding of the physical universe in the twentieth century.
(*U.S. Naval Academy*)

PART SIX

◀ The Statue of Liberty, a beacon of faith to Americans and of hope to the oppressed of many lands. (*The New York Port Authority*)

The Golden Door

FROM COLONIAL TIMES the Jews of America, largely Sephardic or Germanic in origin, had become intimately woven into the fabric of the red, white, and blue. More and more of them rose to positions of distinction, enhancing all phases of their country's life, not only in peace but in war. By the 1880s the native-born, or nearly native-born, American Jew was a vital part of the great American landscape. Antisemitism, sporadic in Christian America, was at a reasonable low, and while the rich went to banks, the poor went to synagogues. The Jewish future was assured under the Stars and Stripes.

Events in nineteenth-century Russia, however, were to alter the complacent face of American Jewry in unexpected ways. In 1881 Alexander II, czar of all the Russias, was assassinated by terrorists, and the Jews were blamed. The Jews of Eastern Europe, several million of them, were accused of also causing bad weather, severe droughts, famines, plagues, and falling stock-market prices. Within a few days Alexander III, a young man of limited education and less intelligence, succeeded his fallen father. Under the influence of his tutor, Konstantin Pobyedonostzev, the procurator of the holy synod of the Orthodox Church, Alexander undertook a campaign of antisemitic violence that shocked the civilized world. The Pobyedonostzev plan was exquisite in its clarity: The pogroms unleashed in Russia and in Russian-controlled territory, which included much of Poland and Rumania, would ensure the emigration of a third of the Jews; another third would accept

Ellis Island, the main entry point for new immigrants, as it looked in the 1890s. (*U.S. National Park Service*)

baptism, and the remaining third would be starved to death or otherwise eliminated. Holy Mother Russia had declared war on the Jews, and the year 1881 became a turning point in American Jewish history as momentous as 1492, when Ferdinand and Isabella decreed the expulsion from Spain.

From Vilna in the north to Warsaw and Kiev and on to Odessa in the south, Jewish centers of learning and culture were attacked; *shtetlach*, or Jewish villages, were destroyed; and Jews themselves were insulted, humiliated, and killed. From 1881 to 1920 more than 2 million Yiddish-speaking Jews fled to our shores. These hapless and woebegone victims of Mother Russia almost quadrupled the existing population of Jewish America. Their predecessors, the German Jews, deeply embarrassed by the shabby appearance of their backward brethren, offered little more than patronizing advice and a bar of soap. The *goyim,* or gentiles, shunned the strange creatures, with their beards, curling sideburns, and yarmulkes, or treated them as less than human. Yet despite American resistance, these same Jews, having passed through the golden door, brought this country a unique burst of creative energy and enterprise, the like of which had not been seen for many generations.

Sickened by the long sea voyage and apprehensive of the future, the new immigrants arrived at Ellis Island with little baggage, a distrust of government, faith in their ancient God, and a monumental ignorance of American ways. Steerage conditions had been foul, "the filth and stench almost unendurable." For the ship companies, cheap was always cheap, and a profit had to be turned. Pork was often announced as the main meal when the ship's officers knew full well that their Jewish passengers would not eat it; a penny saved was a penny earned.

Ellis Island, opened in 1892 as the national immigration center for incoming aliens, was the gateway to the land where the streets were paved with gold and all men were created equal. Since new arrivals were tested for medical reasons and political beliefs, anxiety and panic gripped the voyagers; a Jewish commentator of the period likened it to the Day of Judgment, "when we have to prove our fitness to enter Heaven."

In the main building the immigrants were received by American officials who shouted and ordered them about in an unknown language, English. Doctors raced them up and downstairs, marched them around in circles, and poked their private parts with rubber-gloved fingers. Those who passed the medical examination were then confronted by the legal inspectors, who felt strongly about the answers to three questions: "Are you an anarchist?" "Are you a polygamist?" "Do you have a criminal record?" Fortunately the ordeal lasted for only a few days. For the many who were to become new Americans, there was celebration; for the others, despair: A return to Europe was directed; suicide on the voyage back was not uncommon.

Towering over Ellis Island and in full view of the intimidated immigrants was the colossal Statue of Liberty, dedicated in 1886 on nearby Bedloe's Island. In the pedestal of our most famous national monument was inscribed a sonnet, the words of which still ring through this land of liberty:

Keep, ancient lands, your storied pomp! cries she,
With silent lips. Give me your tired, your poor,
Your huddled masses, yearning to breathe free,
The wretched refuse of your teeming shore,
Send these, the homeless, tempest-tossed to me.
I lift my lamp beside the golden door!

Steerage immigrants coming on deck to check their belongings and for a breath of fresh air. (*UPI*)

Arrivals at Ellis Island awaiting processing. (*Amalgamated Clothing Workers of America, New York City*)

An anonymous East European immigrant, one of the hundreds of thousands to pass muster at Ellis Island by the turn of the century. (*The New York Public Library*)

An Italian organ grinder entertaining Jewish street kids for pennies on the Lower East Side in 1899. The organ grinder was a double amputee. (*The New-York Historical Society*)

The Yiddish immigrants would have been astonished to learn that the poem, only part of which is quoted, was written by an American Jew, the talented Emma Lazarus; that her father, Moses Lazarus, was a founder of the Knickerbocker Club in Manhattan, which became one of the most exclusive gentile clubs in America; and that the Wall Street Jews strenuously objected to the term "The wretched refuse," believing it was directed at them.

Among the German and Irish immigrants of the urban ghettos, the hordes of "Yids" were welcomed with less than kindness and even in the boondocks, where a Jew was rarely seen, antisemitism was reaching fever pitch. Heaven was not to be as advertised. Antisemitic incidents became commonplace, but none tarnished the image of America more than the events leading to the murder of Leo Frank.

Frank, who was reared in Brooklyn, the sensitive son of immigrant parents, was convicted of murder in Georgia in 1913 and subsequently lynched by a redneck mob; the Leo Frank case represents the most outrageous display of antisemitism in this country's history.

On April 26, 1913, the battered body of a fourteen-year-old girl was found on the basement floor of a small Atlanta pencil factory managed by the twenty-nine-year-old Leo Frank. Frank, happily married and a respected member of the Atlanta Jewish community, was accused of the brutal murder and probable rape. At his trial enraged mobs crowded the courthouse area. Men with loaded rifles stood outside the courthouse windows and, pointing their weapons at the judge and jury, chanted over and over, "Hang the Jew, hang the Jew." Thomas Watson, the anti-Jewish, antiblack,

Emma Lazarus, the American Jew who wrote the famous Statue of Liberty sonnet. (*American Jewish Archives, Cincinnati*)

and anti-Catholic publisher of a Georgia newspaper noted for its bigotry, offered choice wisdom to the mob. "Every student of sociology knows," he shouted, "that the nigra's lust for the white woman is not much fiercer than the lust of the licentious Jew for the gentile." So impressed were the folks down in Georgia with their fount of true wisdom that they later elected Tom Watson to the U.S. Senate.

The crowds at the trial were whipped to near frenzy by the likes of Watson and Hugh Dorsey, the prosecuting attorney, who in his closing remarks commented on criminals of Jewish ancestry and, denying any prejudice, added that Jews "rise to heights sublime, but also sink to the lowest depths of degradation." It never occurred to Dorsey that Leo Frank, not the Jews, was on trial. But no matter, Hugh Dorsey was to be elected governor of Georgia for his good work in the conviction of Leo Frank. For of course, Frank was found guilty and was sentenced to hanging. Mountain singers expressed the popular feeling with unusual sensitivity in a ballad ending in these lines: "Judge Roan passed the sentence; He passed it very well. The Christian doers of heaven sent Leo Frank to hell."

The "Christian doers of heaven" knew very well that Leo Frank was innocent and that their star witness, Jim Conley, was the murderer of Mary Phagan, but why would they execute another "nigra" when they had trapped a real, live Jew, especially a Yankee Jew? There was no political profit in that.

The bewildered Leo Frank was taken to Milledgeville, a maximum security prison near Macon. Appeals for a new trial dragged on for nearly two years and were denied every step of the way right up to the U.S. Supreme Court. The hanging of Leo Frank was imminent when the governor of Georgia, John M. Slaton, in a move he knew would end his political career, commuted Frank's sentence to life imprisonment. For this courageous act, he was threatened and denounced as "King of the Jews." Armed mobs, determined to kill a Jew, ruled Georgia in the summer of 1915. A few weeks after the commutation thirty redneck vigilantes miraculously gained entry to Milledgeville Prison. Undetected by guards and other officials, the mob dragged Leo Frank from a hospital bed, where he was recovering from stab wounds inflicted by a Jew-hating fellow prisoner, chained him to the back of a car, pulled his broken body over fifty miles of dirt road, and then strung him up. They lynched a corpse, for Frank had died miles before he was delivered to the hanging tree. Not a single one of the vigilantes was ever brought to the bar of justice.

The bewildered Leo Frank on trial for murder in an Atlanta courthouse in 1913. (*Anti-Defamation League of B'nai B'rith, New York City*)

THE MURDER of Leo Frank shocked the American Jewish community, but on the Lower East Side immigrant Jews, conditioned to anti-semitism by the czar's thugs, went about the everyday business of surviving. Undismayed by the harsh realities of their lives, the poverty and sickness, the slums and the filth, the down-town Jews stubbornly insisted on their "Jew-ishness." In the struggle to preserve their rich heritage they created the strongest ethnic culture of its time, the Yiddish American culture. Gifted men and women, in medicine and the sciences, in law, in culture and art, in scholar-ship, in business and industry, were nurtured in the Yiddish American environment.

Naturally there was a dark side to the slum tenements of the Lower East Side: a Jewish underworld. Monk Eastman, Kid Twist, Gyp the

Blood, Big Jack Zelig, Little Augie, Arnold Rothstein, and Benjamin "Bugsy" Siegel were some of the best-known gangsters and racketeers of their time, but none was to surpass Meyer Lansky in notoriety or in criminal creativity. Lansky was definitely not a Leo Frank.

"He would have been chairman of the board of General Motors if he'd gone into legitimate business," an FBI agent once said of Lansky with grudging admiration. Maier Suchowijansky, better known to law enforcement agencies as Meyer Lansky, was born in Grodno, Russia, in 1902 and emigrated to the Lower East Side as a boy of eight with his parents, Yetta and Max.

From an impoverished childhood, Lansky maneuvered his way up through the violent ranks of organized crime, parlaying Prohibition profits into hundreds of illicit and legitimate ventures. Little Meyer, only five feet four inches tall, was a key figure in the 1934 creation of the national crime syndicate, which brought gangland kingdoms into a loosely organized crime empire. He once boasted to an underworld associate, "We're bigger than U.S. Steel." By that time Lansky was a kingpin of the syndicate.

His financial wizardry was legendary. He devised schemes to infiltrate legitimate businesses, set up sophisticated means to skim re-

A street scene, the Lower East Side in 1912; all kinds of ghetto kids, future saints and sinners, grew up on such streets. (*The New York Public Library*)

ceipts and evade taxes, and contrived ingenious plots to hide investments in Florida and Nevada, Cuba, the Bahamas, and Switzerland. From gambling to loan-sharking, banking, and stock manipulation and from there to numbered accounts and real estate, Lansky and his colleagues drew huge profits in illicit enterprises.

In the 1920s he and his partner, Bugsy Siegel, were hired gunmen and enforcers for the mob. They ran floating crap games on the sly and were well known to the police on the Lower East Side as neighborhood toughs. Yet despite a criminal history that spanned more than a half century, Lansky went to jail only once, and that was for two months on a gambling conviction in 1953. Little Meyer had many friends in high places.

"What will be will be," Lansky philosophized in his old age, "a Jew has a slim chance in the world." On his death at eighty-one it was estimated that the immigrant boy from Grodno had amassed a personal fortune of $300 million, most of it tucked away in Swiss bank accounts and hidden investments.

THE WILD SHOUTS of pushcart peddlers echoed through the congested streets of "Jew Town." Hester, Willet, Orchard, Delancey, Rivington, Essex, Ludlow, Suffolk, Division, and Allen were famous streets not only in Manhattan and satellite Jewish neighborhoods in the Bronx and Brooklyn but in Jewish ghettos across the nation. The Lower East Side had become the beacon of Yiddish culture in America.

Intellectuals, poets and playwrights, pastrami cutters, sweatshop workers, wagonmen and *shlepers,* Jews on their way to worship, and street kids everywhere jostled one another on the overcrowded thoroughfares. In the tenement district where many buildings were limited to 75 occupants, 200 Jewish immigrants lived with access to four or five public toilets. Tuberculosis, which was rampant, came to be called the Jewish disease. Thousands of slum Jews, nameless and unremembered, succumbed to the wretchedness of the ghetto, but no matter how desperate living conditions became, the

Meyer Lansky after being questioned by Manhattan police in 1958. Little Meyer was definitely not a Leo Frank. (*UPI*)

new immigrants knew that they had escaped the czars and the Cossacks—and that things would be better for their sons and daughters.

The hope, courage, and intellectual fiber that brought the *shtetl* "Yids" to this strange country in the first place were the exact qualities needed for survival. Yiddish dailies, the likes of which had never before been seen in any ghetto, thundered and pontificated about Jewish problems and the world order. Abraham Cahan, the editor of the *Forward,* issued pronouncements on America, little of which he understood, on antisemitism, which he understood too well; on socialism, the East Side, noisy

Hester Street, the queen of slum streets, in the 1890s. (*The New York Public Library*)

Victrolas, and cockroaches. Under Cahan's imperious leadership the *Forward* became the most important Jewish newspaper in America. The *Tageblatt,* another dominant Yiddish daily, was run by John Paley, a Jew often accused of being a secret Christian by Cahan and the *Forward.* Orthodox in tone, the *Tageblatt* specialized in crime, violence, and pious sex and offered moral precepts to its semiliterate readers. Paley, a clever cynic, was himself a lover of oysters, whiskey, and charming ladies, all *treyf,* or nonkosher, on the Orthodox menu. The *Freiheit,* a newspaper managed by Jewish Communists, flourished in the 1920s and 1930s, explaining the Yiddish world in terms of the class struggle. In the midst of their cheerless lives the readers of the Yiddish press were given madness, sadness, anger, joy, invective, and shining moments that made life bearable.

ENTERTAINMENT, that magical potion for the relief of harsh realities and frustration, found its outlet in the Yiddish theater. During the Depression there were more theaters operating on or near Second Avenue in the Yiddish heartland than on Broadway; the immigrants, no matter how tough the times, always had a few pennies for their beloved theater, flamboyant and vital as it was.

Grand gestures, lofty language, and fancy costumes transmuted gray, leaden audiences into gold. The butcher, the baker, and the sweatshop worker became princes of the royal blood for a few hours; struggling mothers, the backbone of the East Side, were queens; and the unemployed intellectual was suddenly a prime minister or a great scholar. On the stage pomposity and declamation reigned over an audience that was clamorous, highly critical, and

Pushcart peddlers on Essex Street in the 1910s. (*Wide World Photos*)

Ghetto children cele-
brating the Fourth of
July on their fire escape.
(*Amalgamated Clothing
Workers of America, New
York City*)

The Third Avenue el, which connected the Lower East Side with
uptown Manhattan, in 1896; it no longer exists. (*J. & W. Seligman
& Co.*)

Jacob P. Adler, the dominant Yiddish actor of his time. (*American Jewish Archives, Cincinnati*)

starved for glamour. Orange peels, half-eaten sandwiches, and kosher pickles were dumped under seats, and arguments erupted over the quality of the play and the performers. The spectators hissed and shouted Yiddish obscenities at the villain or at any other actor, depending on their mood and the prices they had paid for tickets. It was an Elizabethan audience, alive and involved and often more interesting than the drama itself.

The majestic Jacob P. Adler, the most dominant Yiddish actor of his time, could silence a rowdy audience with a mere entrance. Bold gestures, a commanding presence, and a sterling voice, which carried to the last row of the uppermost balcony, transformed Adler, the young immigrant from Odessa, into the idol of Second Avenue, the Jew who could be king. John Barrymore, Isadora Duncan, and other connoisseurs of the American theater came to see and admire the great Adler, whose conceit by that time had reached astronomical proportions. When he died in 1926, his coffin was reverentially carried from theater to theater on the East Side, while thousands of mourners crowded the

streets. It was a funeral fit for royalty and entirely worthy of Adler himself, who had planned all the details.

Boris Thomashefsky, another star of magnitude, was an actor, a song and dance man, and a Second Avenue folk hero, who reluctantly pandered to a low order of taste in the Yiddish theater. In 1881 the fifteen-year-old Boris came to these shores from Russia and found work in a cigarette factory. He drifted from job to job until he discovered his pot of gold—the immigrant theater. A large, well-built man, Thomashefsky looked splendid in gold tights and enjoyed heroic roles on the stage, though his talent ran to song and dance. Audiences in New York and elsewhere on the eastern seaboard loved his broad style. He was also a tireless producer, a director, and a "doctor" of Yiddish plays of dubious value.

In his early teens, before New York beckoned, Maurice Schwartz was a ragpicker's helper in London. By 1919 the unknown ragpicker had become an esteemed and well-established Second Avenue actor and the director of the distinguished Yiddish Art Theater.

Young and progressive, Schwartz, a vigorous opponent of shlock, attracted talented Yiddish playwrights and actors to his company: the playwrights Peretz Hirshbein, Jacob Gordin, David Pinski, and Ossip Dymov and the players Jacob Ben Ami, Joseph Buloff, Celia Adler, Ludwig Satz, Bertha Gersten. Over three decades Schwartz's Yiddish Art Theater produced original plays and Yiddish translations of Molière, Chekhov, Shaw, Gorky, and Schnitzler. An American critic once wrote of Schwartz's company that it "is the noblest theatrical enterprise in New York."

Yiddish theater, at its best, was to influence the American stage for decades to come; crossbreeding is often the best breeding.

Maurice Schwartz, the distinguished founder of the Yiddish Art Theater. (*American Jewish Archives, Cincinnati*)

Boris Thomashefsky, a Second Avenue folk hero. (*American Jewish Archives, Cincinnati*)

JEWISH SOCIALISM, which found its finest expression in the American labor movement, appeared on the Lower East Side at the turn of the century. The appalling conditions of the sweatshop, where work often began at six in the morning and continued till ten at night, where sanitation was foul and a menace to public health, and where workers averaged a weekly salary of about $7, brought on bitter and violent strikes.

Morris Hillquit, an immigrant Jew from Latvia, was until his death in 1933 a dominant figure in American socialism and a champion of labor. Hillquit, a believer in the electoral process, was a candidate twice for mayor of New York City and five times for congressman. Although he drew substantial numbers of votes—250,000 Jews lived on the East Side then—he never won a race.

As a youth Samuel Gompers, another immigrant Jew, worked as a cigarmaker in a tenement sweatshop. By the 1880s he had become a labor leader of some renown. An opponent of socialism and defender of freewheeling capitalism, Gompers was a reformer rather than a radical. He gained national prominence in 1886, when he founded the American Federation of Labor (AFL) and was elected its first president, a position he held until his death in 1924. Morris Hillquit, the socialist intellectual, often criticized Gompers, the monarch of organized labor. Charges and countercharges filled the fetid air of union halls, but the sweatshop system went on.

The tragic Triangle Shirtwaist Company fire, a momentous event in American labor history, was to mark the beginning of the end of ghetto sweatshops in New York, Boston, Philadelphia, Chicago, and Cincinnati. After years of strikes and confrontations, it took a cruel disaster to penetrate the profit-minded American conscience. In the spring of 1911 Triangle, one of the largest garment sweat-labor factories in Manhattan, burst into flames. Within twenty minutes 146 workers, most of them Jewish and Italian girls, trapped by the

A strike against sweatshops in New York City in the 1910s. (*Amalgamated Clothing Workers of America, New York City*)

President Woodrow Wilson and Samuel Gompers, the Jewish immigrant who founded the American Federation of Labor, at a meeting in 1916. (*American Jewish Archives, Cincinnati*)

fire, were burned or jumped to their death. The Lower East Side exploded. Mass meetings were held; hysteria ruled, photographs of the charred bodies were displayed; the Yiddish press raged, and militancy came sharply forward. Enough was enough, even for the ghetto poor.

Rose Schneiderman, the young and fiery leader of the Women's Trade Union League and one of the outstanding labor unionists of her time, mesmerized audiences with her eloquence when she shouted, "This is not the first time girls have been burned alive in this city. Every week I must learn of the untimely death of one of my sister workers. Every year thousands of us are maimed. The life of men and women is so cheap and property is so sacred!"

The *Forward,* under the gifted Abraham Cahan, printed fierce editorials and touching memorial poems, one of which ended with the lines:

This is our funeral,
These our graves,
Our children. . . .

With typical insensitivity rich uptown Jews, alarmed by increasing radicalism in the ghetto, warned that the image of American Jews would be tarnished if Jewish concerns "fell into the hands of radical theorists whose vagaries will then be accepted by the American nation as expressive of the views and the intentions of the *whole* Jewish community."

Undismayed by upper-crust Jewish criticism, workers on the East Side launched an attack on the sweatshop system; they were in no mood for Uncle Tomism. Spearheaded by the Amalgamated Clothing Workers of America—led by Sidney Hillman, one of the founders of the CIO and later an adviser to Franklin Roosevelt, and by Jacob Potofsky, an intellectual of stature—and by the International Ladies' Garment Workers' Union—under the strong leadership of David Dubinsky, who as a youth had escaped from a political prison in Siberia and made his way to America—the sweatshop system, after years of struggle, ended. It is commonly agreed that the Jewish labor movement was remarkably fortunate in the intellectual caliber of its leadership, more so, indeed, than the American labor movement in general.

IMMIGRANT JEWS, during the years of deprivation, generated a phenomenal drive to succeed in their new homeland, a creative force they passed on to their children and grandchildren. Up from the streets, the ghettos, and the

New York City police breaking up a labor demonstration in the 1920s. (*The New York Public Library*)

sweatshops they rose by the thousands, and antisemitism dogged their every step. Henry Ford, a leading American antisemite, claimed that the economy of the country was held in pawn by the Jews and that "international Jewish bankers" controlled the destiny of Christendom. The specters conjured up by Ford and his ilk were not without effect on certain Jewish leaders, who offered their brethren a variety of advice: that more of them should go into farming and the handicrafts, shun the commercial and professional callings, curtail their participation in government service, and forgo positions of conspicuous honor and public trust. In short, American Jews were to stay in the closet until the Messiah appeared or antisemitism disappeared, whichever came first. The immigrants took little notice of the well-meaning if obtuse instruction.

In two generations the Jewish immigrants from Eastern Europe and their offspring had made an enormous advance in their economic status. Sweat labor was unionized, pushcart peddlers became retail merchants and entrepreneurs, and the owners of sweatshops went into real estate. Their children and grandchildren came to occupy positions of responsibility in the commercial, industrial, and professional life of the country, besides making notable contributions to its scientific, legal, cultural, and artistic progress. The fundamental democratic tradition of America had enabled them to find the level to which their abilities entitled them. And in the final analysis, they became prosperous because the country as a whole became prosperous.

Zionism, the dream of a reestablished Jewish nation in ancient Palestine, met with little success among nineteenth-century American Jews, and even in the ghettos immigrants were much more interested in socialism and the labor movement than in sectarian Jewish nationalism. The idea of a Jewish homeland, the center of a scattered nation, had not yet found its time. It took monumental sacrifice and tragedy before the dream became reality.

In 1914 Louis Dembitz Brandeis, a lawyer of great stature, became the leader of American Zionism, a Jewish political movement then without head or tail. Born in 1856 in Louisville, Kentucky, Brandeis, a graduate of Harvard Law School and a prominent Boston attorney, was the only American Jew of his time who could unite uptown and downtown Jews. As an arbitrator in the violent garment industry strikes of the early 1900s he gained the trust and respect of the ghetto radicals even while the uptown Jews considered him one of their own. When he was asked how he could be an American and a Zionist at the same time, Brandeis, a master of the pithy comment, replied, "Multiple loyalties are objectionable only if they are inconsistent."

His legal arguments in the public interest, especially before the U.S. Supreme Court, brought him the highest respect from jurists and the title of the People's Attorney from journalists. In 1916 Brandeis was appointed to the U.S. Supreme Court by President Woodrow Wilson, despite the strenuous objections of financial and utility interests.

Another pioneer American Zionist was Henrietta Szold, an earnest young teacher of immigrant Jews, who founded Hadassah in 1912; today it is the most important Zionist organization in America. Her tireless and inspirational efforts on behalf of the neglected poor and sick of Palestine, irrespective of race or creed, led to the establishment of an imposing array of hospitals, clinics, and child welfare centers in the ancient homeland. As a girl Henrietta had learned the humanitarian lessons of her distinguished father, Rabbi Benjamin Szold of Baltimore, one of the few American clergymen invited to march behind the casket of the slain Abraham Lincoln.

Through Youth Aliyah, a group largely supported by funds from Hadassah, the elderly Henrietta Szold saved thousands of Jewish children and orphans from the hands of the Nazis. She will long be revered as a saint by her host of followers.

Centuries-old antisemitism in Europe, fueled by the church and stoked by the very nature of institutionalized Christianity, which demands a devil in its Passion play, finally erupted in Germany and other European nations in the 1930s. In an act of genocide, unparalleled in

Louis D. Brandeis, the labor lawyer who became an
outstanding U.S. Supreme Court justice. (*American
Jewish Archives, Cincinnati*)

Henrietta Szold, the Baltimore-born Zionist and founder of Hadassah. (*Hadassah, New York City*)

human history, the Nazis and their collaborators brutally and systematically exterminated 6 million European Jews, while the gentile world stood by, uttering sympathetic noises. American Jews, uptown and downtown, from New York to San Francisco, were stunned into silence, a rare occurrence among Jews. Commissions and delegations were dispatched to Washington in an attempt to turn the course of human events in Germany, without success. Congress was indifferent; the Jewish organizations were ineffectual; the State Department's Jewish Division, under Assistant Secretary of State Breckenridge Long, was antisemitic; and President Franklin D. Roosevelt, politically callous.

Israel, child of the Holocaust, was born of bloodshed and pain after the Second World War, and even American Jews who had opposed Zionism celebrated the birth of the new Jewish state, an event of such proportions that the post-Nazi remnants of world Jewry regarded it with the awesome respect reserved only for the building of Solomon's Temple, of much more ancient times. To most American Jews the continuing survival of Israel against a ring of enemies has all the semblance of a biblical miracle. And while their allegiance belongs to America, few would deny the surge of heart and spirit that the birth of a proud Israel brought into their lives.

It would take a work of encyclopedic magnitude and forbidding proportions to encompass the roster of immigrant Jews and their offspring who became notable Americans after the 1880s. Their creative energy and drive to success earned them positions of high distinction in government and public service, industry and commerce, science and medicine, law, literature, music, the fine arts, the theater, sports, education, and still other spheres. This modest panorama unfortunately must forgo comprehensiveness and, at the risk of disagreement and even harsh criticism, confine itself to naming and picturing only a few of the many Jews whose special contributions have enriched American life.

Louis D. Brandeis, already mentioned in these pages, Benjamin Nathan Cardozo, and Felix Frankfurter were among that rare company of judges who influenced the course of American jurisprudence. Cardozo, a brilliant Columbia University graduate, became chief judge of the New York State Court of Appeals, which, largely through his intellectual leadership, gained international fame. In 1932 he was appointed to the U.S. Supreme Court by President Herbert Hoover to succeed Oliver Wendell Holmes. Cardozo, one of the foremost spokesmen for a changing law in a changing society,

was a philosopher of law and probably the most influential American judge of his time.

Felix Frankfurter, a graduate of the City College of New York, was appointed professor of law at Harvard, a position he held for twenty-five years. His voice reached far beyond the narrow academic world, and he was asked to serve on special government committees, becoming one of the architects of the New Deal. President Franklin Roosevelt appointed Frankfurter to the Supreme Court in 1939. While on the high bench, the former law professor, a man of liberal tendencies, proved to be an advocate of judicial restraint; he consistently gave the benefit of the doubt to legislation limiting civil liberties, believing that the government has a right to protect itself through investigating committees and legislation and that the Court must exercise self-restraint in interfering with the popular will as expressed by its representatives in the Congress.

On the streets of New York and elsewhere Jewish kids by the hundreds sought out show business as their avenue to success. While their

Yad Vashem, Jerusalem, the eternal light memorial to the 6 million who died. (*The Government of Israel*)

President Harry S Truman accepts a sacred Torah scroll
from Chaim Weizmann, first president of Israel, at the
White House in 1948. (*The Government of Israel*)

mothers nagged them about becoming busi-
nessmen, lawyers, accountants, and doctors, the
youngsters, more aware of the brutality of
ghetto life than their parents were, dreamed
of careers in vaudeville, that great arena of pleasure, with its gilded theaters, easy money and
fame, far from sweatshops, soapbox orators,
slum tenements, and a wide range of Jewish
woes. So far as it concerned them, the young
and future entertainers felt that their parents,
older immigrant Jews, were sweating away their
lives in toil and hardship in a rich land. The
bitter generational conflict that developed between immigrant traditionalists and their eager
Americanized children was surely not confined

to the ghetto or to young Jewish entertainers.

Al Jolson, one of the most popular entertainers of his time, was born in Kiev, the son
of an Orthodox father. He spent his childhood
in Washington, D.C., but in his early teens
made his way to the Lower East Side, where
he sang in saloons, despite condemnations by
his father. *The Jazz Singer,* Hollywood's first talking motion picture, starred Jolson and was
loosely based on his life.

The list of pioneer Jewish entertainers—
singers, dancers, and comics—is long and distinguished, and the names of Fanny Brice, Eddie Cantor, Sophie Tucker, Jack Benny, the
Marx Brothers, Milton Berle, and the incom-

Benjamin Nathan Cardozo, appointed to the U.S. Supreme Court by President Herbert Hoover to succeed the great Oliver Wendell Holmes. (*American Jewish Archives, Cincinnati*)

Felix Frankfurter, another learned Jewish Supreme
Court justice. (*American Jewish Archives, Cincinnati*)

Al Jolson, one of the most popular entertainers of his time, on the set of *The Jazz Singer* in 1927. From left to right, Darryl Zanuck; Jack Warner, the studio producer; Jolson, the star; and Warner Oland, the makers of Hollywood's first talking motion picture. (*Warner Bros.*)

parable George Burns will long be remembered in the annals of American show business.

Though they are the butt of endless jokes and coarse anecdotes, the penniless Jewish youths, the restless and sharp hustlers who founded the largest and most successful film industry in the world remain the most colorful of Jewish immigrant tycoons. The names of Carl Laemmele, Samuel Goldwyn, Louis B. Mayer, William Fox, the Warner brothers, the Schenks, the Selznicks, Harry Cohn, Jesse Lasky, and Adolph Zukor still echo through Hollywood's corridors of power, even as the capital of filmmaking is slurred as "Ollavoood."

In the 1950s the House Un-American Activities Committee, then in the hands of professional anti-Communists, launched an unwarranted attack on Hollywood. It marked the periodic swing of the American pendulum to superpatriotism and bigotry, the worst kind of Americanism and the heavy-handed enemy of creativity. Film careers were damaged or destroyed by the committee, while the movie moguls, those pioneer Jewish princes, fled for cover. Dorothy Parker, herself Jewish and a famous wit, commented, in defense of the studios, that "the only 'ism' Hollywood believes in is plagiarism."

Eddie Cantor, one of vaudeville's greatest song-and-dance men. (*American Jewish Archives, Cincinnati*)

The wistful Groucho Marx, star of the Marx Brothers team, whose zany and anarchic humor won national audiences for years. (*The New York Public Library*)

Among the earliest movie stars of Jewish origin were Charlie Chaplin, born in London to the Thornstein family, and Douglas Fairbanks, born Douglas Ullman in Denver, the son of a Jewish father. Emanuel Goldenberg, known to his millions of fans as Edward G. Robinson, was a Rumanian immigrant, and Paul Muni, the finest character actor of his time, had been a star of the Yiddish stage under his true name, Muni Weisenfreund. Cecil B. De Mille, who long hid his Jewish roots, ironically became the world's most famous director of biblical film epics.

Of more recent celebration in the world of feature filmmaking is a myriad of actors and directors of American Jewish descent: Woody Allen, Edward Asner, Lauren Bacall, Martin Balsam, Richard Benjamin, Mel Brooks, Tony Curtis, Kirk Douglas, Joel Grey, Goldie Hawn, Dustin Hoffman, Jack Klugman, Michael Landon, Jerry Lewis, Sidney Lumet, Walter Matthau, Paul Newman, Mike Nichols, Tony Randall, George Segal, Steven Spielberg, Barbra Streisand, Shelley Winters, and many, many others.

Jack Benny, one of America's favorite comedians, and his wife, Mary Livingstone, in 1939. (*Chamberlain & Brown Theatrical Agency*)

Fanny Brice, starring at
New York's Palace
Theater in the 1920s. (*The
New York Public Library*)

George Burns, the last of the great
Lower East Side cowboys. (*The New
York Public Library*)

Louis B. Mayer, a founder of Metro-Goldwyn-Mayer, in the 1930s. When Mayer died, Goldwyn, his former partner, commented on the large funeral with the words "Give the public what it wants and it comes out in crowds." (*American Jewish Archives, Cincinnati*)

Mr. and Mrs. Samuel Goldwyn in 1933. Goldwyn, born Goldfish in Poland, arrived in America when he was fourteen and became one of Hollywood's greatest producers. (*New York Morning Telegraph*)

The creative contribution of American Jews to the Broadway stage can only be described as massive. Their ventures in this hazardous realm have been bold and imaginative, and the expansion of the American theater would hardly have been possible without the ingenuity and daring of pioneers like Charles and Daniel Frohman, the Schuberts, Abraham Erlanger, Sam Harris, the Nederlanders, Florenz Ziegfeld, and the great David Belasco, whose story has been called the story of the American stage. A theater owner, producer, playwright, and sometime actor, Belasco was born in San Francisco in 1853, shortly after the gold rush. He was actively connected with the theater from his youth and as a teenager was the stage manager of theaters in Virginia City, Nevada,

Charlie Chaplin, Mary Pickford, and
Douglas Fairbanks, the brightest of
early movie stars, having fun in the
1920s. Both Chaplin and Fairbanks
were of Jewish origin. (*United Artists
Corporation*)

and in San Francisco. His association with the
Frohmans brought him to New York, and by
1895 he was recognized as an independent producer of creative power. His detailed and lavish
stage settings became world-famous vehicles
for his performers; Belasco enjoyed being a star
maker. His spectacular success made him
Broadway's leading light by the 1920s.

David Merrick, of more recent times, was
born in St. Louis and continued the Belasco
tradition with hit after commercial hit. His un-
paralleled theatrical career can best be illus-
trated by his productions of *Look Back in Anger,
A Taste of Honey, Becket, Luther, Marat/Sade, The
Entertainer, One Flew over the Cuckoo's Nest, Hello,
Dolly!, Gypsy, 42nd Street,* and many others. *42nd
Street* was David Merrick's eighty-fourth
Broadway production.

Harold Prince, born in New York City and
educated at the University of Pennsylvania, is
a sensitive producer-director with credits for
The Pajama Game, Damn Yankees, West Side Story,

A Funny Thing Happened on the Way to the Forum, Fiddler on the Roof, Cabaret, Zorba, Company, Evita, Sweeney Todd, and other Broadway hits.

Joseph Papp, born Papirofsky in Brooklyn, has become one of the outstanding theatrical producers of modern times. His creativity is expressed in the many productions of Shakespeare staged by his company, the New York Shakespeare Festival; in the Public Theatre, which Papp founded in 1967 to encourage new talent and new ideas; and in his development of hits such as *Hair, Sticks and Bones, That Championship Season, For Colored Girls . . . , The Pirates of Penzance,* and *A Chorus Line,* the longest-running play in Broadway history. Papp was the producer of Pulitzer Prize-winning plays in 1970, 1973, and 1976.

As playwrights American Jews began to contribute to the stage in the early nineteenth century: Isaac Harby and Mordecai Manuel Noah have already appeared in these pages. Years later the work of scores of Jewish playwrights had been produced on Broadway, and the plays of many of them—Elmer Rice, Sidney Kingsley, Lillian Hellman, Clifford Odets, Arthur Miller, and others—have become part of the enduring dramatic literature of America. In a lighter vein, George S. Kaufman, Moss Hart, and Neil Simon have also made contributions to the modern stage.

Clifford Odets became an actor and writer after graduating from high school. In 1931, when he was twenty-five, he joined the Group Theatre, organized by Harold Clurman, Cheryl Crawford, and Lee Strasberg, who wished to establish a permanent company that would present contemporary plays of social significance. At its height between 1935 and 1937, the Group produced *Waiting for Lefty, Awake and Sing,* and *Golden Boy,* all written by Odets.

Edward G. Robinson in the 1930 film classic *Little Caesar.* Robinson, born Goldenberg in Rumania, made gangster movies popular in America. (*Cinema Magazine*)

Paul Muni, the finest character actor of his time, in 1955, when he starred in the Broadway production of *Inherit the Wind*. (*The New York Public Library*)

Titans of the modern stage, in the late 1920s: from left to right, David Belasco, who always affected clerical garb; Constantin Stanislavsky, cofounder of the Moscow Art Theatre; and Max Reinhardt, the great Austrian producer and director. Both Belasco and Reinhardt were of Jewish descent. (*The New York Public Library*)

Cecil B. De Mille, the world's most famous director of biblical film epics, was of Jewish origin. (*Paramount Pictures*)

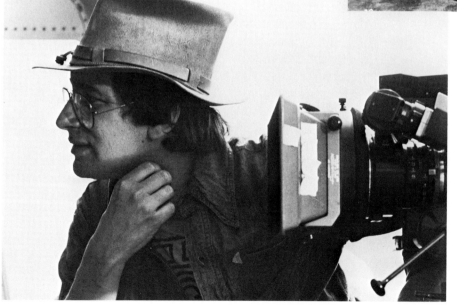

Steven Spielberg, a film director of rare talent, has won critical acclaim as well as popular success for movies such as *Jaws* and *E.T.* (*Columbia Pictures*)

Dustin Hoffman, a powerful and gifted American actor, in *Kramer vs. Kramer.* (*Columbia Pictures*)

Paul Newman, the distinguished actor and director, one of the finest American film talents. (*Warner Bros.*)

Barbra Streisand, the well-known singer, actress, writer, director, and producer. (*American Jewish Archives, Cincinnati*)

The youthful David Merrick, Broadway's most successful producer, on his way to a wedding. (*The New York Public Library*)

Joseph Papp, a celebrated theatrical producer, highly respected for his new approaches to the American stage. (*The New York Public Library*)

Harold Prince, the producer-director, and his friend Stephen Sondheim, the composer-lyricist, at a Broadway opening. (*ASCAP*)

Clifford Odets, an outstanding American dramatist, the golden boy of the 1930s' Group Theatre. (*The New York Public Library*)

George S. Kaufman, the wittiest of American playwrights, in the 1940s. (*American Jewish Archives, Cincinnati*)

Arthur Miller, one of the great modern dramatists, relaxing on a summer's day in the 1950s. (*American Jewish Archives, Cincinnati*)

Neil Simon, the contemporary and successful Broadway playwright, well known for his comedic talents. (*The New York Public Library*)

The company was recognized as a vital theatrical force in its day, and its influence is still felt. Odets, who came to be regarded as the most gifted of American protest dramatists, turned later in life from social drama to turgid and self-conscious plays about individuals caught in personal webs.

George S. Kaufman, born in Pittsburgh, collaborated on more than forty plays, which varied in mood from rowdy farces to sophisticated comedies. Many of his plays were tremendous successes and represent commercial Broadway at its best. Some of his hits were *The Royal Family, Dinner at Eight, Stage Door, Of Thee I Sing,* and, with Moss Hart, *You Can't Take It with You* and *The Man Who Came to Dinner.* Moss Hart, reared in the Bronx, wrote several musicals, including *Face the Music* and *Lady in the Dark.*

One of the greatest American dramatists of the twentieth century is Arthur Miller, brought up in Brooklyn and educated at the University of Michigan. His first important work, *All My Sons,* created a critical sensation and brought Miller to the attention of the intelligent theatergoing public. His next play, *Death of a Salesman,* is regarded as his masterpiece and a landmark in American drama; tragic and powerful, it is the story of an ordinary man relentlessly destroyed by the shallow values he lives by. *The Crucible,* a dramatization of the Salem witch trials, and *A View from the Bridge,* an evocative drama about an Italian family in Brooklyn, are among Miller's many other fine works.

Music, the handmaiden of Jewish liturgy in the Old World, left the sacred for the secular in the New. Aaron Copland, Leonard Bernstein, and George Gershwin have been among those serious composers whose works inspired a fresh musical tradition in America.

Aaron Copland, born in Brooklyn in 1900, is a symphonist and composer of many talents whose American character is evident in his métier. His ballets *Billy the Kid, Rodeo,* and *Appalachian Spring* are outstanding achievements of Americana, as is his chamber piece *John Henry.* Copland, a brilliant innovator, composed the music for the films *Of Mice and Men, Our Town,* and *The Heiress* but will be remembered for his orchestral works *El Salón Mexico,* the Third Symphony, and the *Canticle of Freedom.*

Leonard Bernstein, the composer, conductor, and teacher, was born in Lawrence, Massachusetts, in 1918. The works of this highly versatile musician show remarkable range, from symphonic music, song cycles, chamber pieces, and ballets, such as *Fancy Free,* to an opera, *Trouble in Tahiti,* and several Broadway musicals, including *On the Town, Candide,* and *West Side Story.* For several years Bernstein was the esteemed conductor of the New York Philharmonic Orchestra.

The most popular of the serious American composers was George Gershwin, born in Brooklyn in 1898. After an elementary school education and some musical training he went to work for a music publishing company as a pianist; he was then fifteen. From this humble, nondescript beginning came one of America's premier composers. His principal larger compositions are *Rhapsody in Blue,* an outstanding example of symphonic jazz; the Piano Concerto in F; *An American in Paris,* a tone poem of extraordinary originality; Three Preludes, for the piano; and the timeless *Porgy and Bess,* a folk opera about black life in the South. Gershwin,

a composer of great energy and talent, wrote many popular songs, including "The Man I Love," "I Got Rhythm," "Our Love Is Here to Stay," and "They Can't Take That Away from Me." His brilliant scores for Broadway musicals are still celebrated in *Lady, Be Good, Funny Face, Strike Up the Band, Girl Crazy,* and *Of Thee I Sing.* Gershwin's glittering career ended in 1937, when he was struck down by a cerebral hemorrhage; he was thirty-nine years old. His brother, Ira, the college graduate in the family, was a lyricist of unusual accomplishment, writing the words for his brother's songs and for the songs of other composers of stature. Harold Arlen, Aaron Copland, and Jerome Kern were among his collaborators. In 1932 Ira won a Pulitzer Prize for his lyrics to *Of Thee I Sing.*

For decades the field of popular music was dominated by American Jews, whose songs became standards that are still sung. Jewish com-

Aaron Copland, the gifted composer and founder of a new musical tradition in America. (*ASCAP*)

Leonard Bernstein, composer, conductor, and brilliant musician, performing with his usual verve. (*The New York Philharmonic*)

Ira Gershwin and his younger brother, George, working on a musical in the early 1930s; George Gershwin will long be remembered as one of America's leading composers. (*ASCAP*)

posers and lyricists, the songwriters, were not only legion but remarkable. Irving Berlin, the King of Tin Pan Alley, was born in Russia but arrived on the Lower East Side when he was five. He enjoyed two years of elementary school education, and his father, a cantor, provided his earliest musical training. As a young teenager Berlin worked as a song plugger, a singing waiter in Chinatown, and a vaudeville entertainer. His piano playing was far less than competent, but his ability to create a popular song, a commercial success, was without parallel. He wrote the words and music for more than 1,000 American songs. "Alexander's Ragtime Band," written in 1911, was Berlin's first big hit and served as a ragtime prototype. His Broadway musicals include *As Thousands Cheer, This Is the Army, Annie Get Your Gun, Miss Liberty, Call Me Madam,* and *Mr. President.* Outstanding among Berlin's film scores are those for *Top Hat, Holiday Inn, Blue Skies,* and *There's No Business Like Show Business.* Berlin, the Jewish immigrant boy from Russia, will long be remembered as the creator of "Easter Parade," "White Christmas," and "God Bless America."

Harold Arlen, from Buffalo, New York, sang in a synagogue choir when he was seven; his father was the cantor. By fifteen he was a professional pianist, playing vaudeville theaters and nightclubs. One of America's finest blues composers, he has worked with outstanding lyricists, such as Johnny Mercer, Ira Gershwin, Dorothy Fields, and even Truman Capote. Arlen's Broadway stage scores include *Bloomer Girl,*

Two giants of popular American music, in the early 1930s: George Gershwin and Irving Berlin. (*ASCAP*)

Irving Berlin, the King of Tin Pan Alley, in the 1940s;
Berlin has more commercial hits to his credit than any
other songwriter in history. (*ASCAP*)

Harold Arlen, seated under the umbrella, and his accountant in the 1950s, celebrating the success of "Stormy Weather." (*ASCAP*)

House of Flowers, Saratoga, and *Free and Easy,* a blues opera. Arlen, who has excelled in composing for films, wrote the scores for *The Wizard of Oz, Cabin in the Sky,* and *A Star Is Born.* Among his many song hits are "I Gotta Right to Sing the Blues," "It's Only a Paper Moon," "Stormy Weather," "Blues in the Night," "That Old Black Magic," and "Over the Rainbow."

Jerome Kern, born and reared in New York City, studied musical composition in Germany and England. He wrote operettas and musicals, including *Sally, Sunny, Roberta,* and, with Oscar Hammerstein II, his most enduring work, *Show Boat,* which was first produced in 1927. "Smoke Gets in Your Eyes," "Lovely to Look At," "Ol' Man River," "The Last Time I Saw Paris," and "Can't Help Lovin' Dat Man" are a few of his

memorable compositions. Dorothy Fields, one of Kern's main collaborators and the daughter of comedian Lew Fields, was born in Allenhurst, New Jersey. She became the greatest woman lyricist of her day. Her songs, written with a variety of composers, include "I Can't Give You Anything but Love, Baby," "On the Sunny Side of the Street," "I'm in the Mood for Love," "A Fine Romance," and "Just the Way You Look Tonight."

Richard Rodgers, the brilliant composer of musicals, was born in New York City and studied at Columbia University, where he met both Lorenz ("Larry") Hart and Oscar Hammerstein II, two of the most talented lyricists this country has ever known. Rodgers and Hart began collaborating in 1919, and their musical suc-

Holding hands in a Hollywood nightclub in the 1930s: left to right, Jerome Kern, the composer of *Show Boat;* Dorothy Fields, the great lyricist; and George Gershwin. (*ASCAP*)

Richard Rodgers, at the piano, and Larry Hart in the 1930s; the team of Rodgers and Hart was famous for its wit, mood, and style. (*ASCAP*)

cesses were many: *The Girl Friend, A Connecticut Yankee, On Your Toes, Babes in Arms, I'd Rather Be Right, The Boys from Syracuse,* and *Pal Joey.* Hart, famous for his witty, literate but always expressive lyrics, worked with Richard Rodgers until 1943, when Hart died of pneumonia. Rodgers and Hart songs would fill a catalogue of hits. "Manhattan," "My Heart Stood Still," "Ten Cents a Dance," "Isn't it Romantic?," "Blue Moon," "My Romance," "My Funny Valentine," "The Lady Is a Tramp," "Bewitched, Bothered and Bewildered," and "There's a Small Hotel" are some of them. Rodgers and Oscar Hammerstein began their collaboration with the tremendously successful *Oklahoma!* and continued to make theatrical history with *Carousel, South Pacific, The King and I, Flower Drum Song,* and *The Sound of Music.* Hammerstein, son of Oscar Hammerstein, the Jewish operatic impresario who made his fortune from a cigar-

Frederick Loewe, seated, and Alan Jay Lerner in the 1960s; Lerner and Loewe gave America many Broadway hits, including *My Fair Lady.* (*ASCAP*)

Oscar Hammerstein II, the enormously successful lyricist, relaxing in Hollywood in the 1950s; Rodgers and Hammerstein began collaborating after the death of Larry Hart and made theatrical history. (*ASCAP*)

making machine, worked with Sigmund Romberg, Rudolf Friml, and Jerome Kern before his long association with Rodgers.

Alan Jay Lerner, the gifted American lyricist and librettist, was born in New York City in 1918 and went to Harvard. Lerner began an association with the Berlin-born composer Frederick Loewe in the 1940s that resulted in such musical successes as *Brigadoon, Paint Your Wagon, Camelot,* and the award-winning film *Gigi. My Fair Lady,* their most successful musical, ran for more than six years on Broadway.

Jule Styne, the composer of many Broadway shows, was born in London but emigrated to America in 1913, when he was eight. He received his musical education at the Chicago College of Music and Northwestern University. He wrote the scores for *High Button Shoes, Gentlemen Prefer Blondes, Gypsy,* and *Funny Girl,* all smash hits. Among Styne's earliest collaborators was

Sammy Cahn, born on the Lower East Side and for years a writer of lyrics. The corpus of Cahn's work is so great that it would cover pages not available to the author. It is enough to say that Cahn's career, spanning several decades, began with "Bei Mir Bist Du Schon" and peaked with Academy Awards for "All the Way," "High Hopes," "Call Me Irresponsible," and "Three Coins in the Fountain."

Stephen Sondheim, the composer-lyricist and a graduate of Williams College, is best known for his lyrics to *West Side Story* and *Gypsy* and as the composer-lyricist of *Company, A Little Night Music,* and *Sweeney Todd.*

Other American composers and lyricists of Jewish origin include Arthur Schwartz, Frank Loesser, Howard Dietz, Adolph Green and Betty Comden, and Harold Rome. In more recent years, Burt Bacharach, Marvin Hamlisch, Sheldon Harnick, Jerry Herman, Billy Joel,

Jule Styne, the brilliant Broadway composer, at the piano, and one of his earliest collaborators, Sammy Cahn, the prolific lyricist, in the 1950s. (*ASCAP*)

Art Garfunkel and Paul Simon, fine folk musicians and composers, the creators of "Mrs. Robinson" and "The Sounds of Silence." (*CBS Inc.*)

Barry Manilow, Paul Simon and Art Garfunkel, and Bob Dylan, the protest singer from Duluth, have made their presence felt.

Alma Gluck, the first in a line of Jewish American opera singers, was born Reba Fiersohn in Rumania in 1884. She was a star soprano at the Metropolitan Opera House for several years before she married another Jewish immigrant, the violinist Efrem Zimbalist. Jan Peerce, Robert Merrill, Roberta Peters, Beverly Sills, and Richard Tucker, one of the Metropolitan's finest tenors, continued the tradition of Jewish American opera singers. Among the many concert virtuosos who emigrated to America have been Jascha Heifetz, Mischa El-

man, Nathan Milstein, and the great pianist Vladimir Horowitz. Of more or less American background are Yehudi Menuhin, Isaac Stern, who was brought here from Russia as an infant, Itzhak Perlman, and Pinchas Zuckerman.

Benny Goodman, the most popular clarinetist of his time, was born of Russian-Jewish parents in Chicago in 1909. He studied music at Hull House, where he had the opportunity to hear most of the outstanding black jazz musicians of the Chicago era. In the 1930s he formed his own orchestra and soon became known as the King of Swing. He organized the Benny Goodman trio, which included Gene Krupa and Teddy Wilson, and then, with the addition of

Bob Dylan, composer and performer, a major figure in the folk protest movement of the 1960s. (*CBS Inc.*)

Lionel Hampton, the Benny Goodman quartet. Goodman, also well known as a classical musician, commissioned works from Belá Bartók, Paul Hindemith, and Aaron Copland.

A long and distinguished Yiddish literary tradition, ornamented with the names of Sholom Aleichem, an authentic genius, I. L. Peretz, Sholem Asch, and Isaac Bashevis Singer, found fertile soil in America. Successors to those authors in the world of American literary fiction include the Nobel laureate Saul Bellow, Bernard Malamud, Norman Mailer, Philip Roth, J. D. Salinger, Joseph Heller, E. L. Doctorow, and the all-but-forgotten Nathanael West. Bellow, born of Russian-Jewish immigrants, grew up in the slums of Montreal and Chicago. He attended the University of Chicago and Northwestern University on scholarships and for years was a professor of English at the University of Chicago. His writings are marked by an intellectual concern for the struggles of the sensitive individual in an indifferent and materialistic society. Bernard Malamud, born in Brooklyn and a graduate of City College, was the son of poor parents. His novels, often bizarre and mysterious, reflect a profound interest in Jewish concerns while never neglecting the silent suffering of the humble.

Jewish painters and sculptors were latecomers to the American art scene largely because

Richard Tucker, a star tenor of the Metropolitan Opera, in the 1950s. (*The New York Public Library*)

Beverly Sills, a great American opera singer and a great lady. (*Edgar Vincent Associates*)

The Israeli-born Itzhak
Perlman, now one of
America's greatest
violinists. (*ICM Artists,
Ltd.*)

The young Jascha Heifetz, according
to many critics, the world's finest
violinist, was born in Vilna but has
spent most of his life in America.
(*American Jewish Archives, Cincinnati*)

Benny Goodman, the
King of Swing, in the
1950s. (*The New York Public
Library, Otto F. Hess Collection*)

Bernard Malamud, the
fine American novelist, in
thoughtful repose.
(*American Jewish Archives,
Cincinnati*)

Saul Bellow, the Nobel Prize laureate, in the 1970s. (*American
Jewish Archives, Cincinnati*)

Ben Shahn, the
Lithuanian-born
American painter, noted
for his social and poetic
realism. (*American Jewish
Archives, Cincinnati*)

Max Weber, the Russian-
born American painter,
who became a celebrated
abstract artist and a
highly respected studio
teacher. (*American Jewish
Archives, Cincinnati*)

A rare photograph of the young Jacob
Epstein at his New York studio;
Epstein became Sir Jacob Epstein, one
of the greatest sculptors of the
twentieth century. (*American Jewish
Archives, Cincinnati*)

The striking Louise Nevelson, the gifted contemporary sculptor, brought up in New York City. (*The Pace Gallery, New York City*)

of objections from their Old World parents, who, while they understood the forms of Yiddish culture, held that art was a gentile pursuit fit only for believers in images. Jo Davidson, from the East Side, was a "loafer" to his ghetto father; Davidson's portrait busts are now world-famous. Jacob Epstein, born in New York, was to become Sir Jacob Epstein, one of the greatest sculptors of his time. Abraham Walkowitz, whose family ran a small business on Delancey Street, William Gropper, William Zorach, Ben Shahn, Max Weber, Raphael and Moses Soyer, Mark Rothko, Larry Rivers, and Louise Nevelson were other American artists to rise above a once-restrictive immigrant milieu.

Benny Leonard, an all-
time boxing great, in the
1920s. (*UPI*)

SPORTS IN THE OLD COUNTRY were reserved for the *goyish* upper class, and it would have been unthinkable, as well as dangerous, for a young Jew to dream of becoming an athlete. His parents and peers reinforced the prohibition with their constant homage to cultural heroes, intellectuals, rabbis. The streets of New York and other cities were to change all that. It would have been a bold prophet who, in the last century, predicted that the children and grandchildren of the new immigrants would take their place among the leading athletes of America and that some of them would be crowned champions of their sports.

In the early decades of this century Jews played a leading role in the sport of boxing. Among those who fought their way to the top of their divisions were Abe Attell, the featherweight champion from 1906 to 1912; Battling Levinsky, light heavyweight champion from 1916 to 1920, and Maxie Rosenbloom, in the same class, from 1930 to 1934. Barney Ross, who was to become a Marine hero at Guadalcanal, was lightweight and welterweight champion in the early 1930s, and Benny Leonard, the most popular Jewish ring idol in America, was lightweight champion from 1917 to 1925. Leonard, considered an all-time great by boxing experts, fought in 209 professional bouts, losing only 5 and those by decision, not knockouts. As champion, he retired undefeated. Max Baer, the heavyweight champion who fought under the Star of David, was of German-Irish stock and definitely not Jewish.

Barney Ross, with his mother, after winning the welterweight championship in 1934; Ross in the Second World War was awarded the Silver Star for heroism at the Battle of Guadalcanal. (*American Jewish Archives, Cincinnati*)

Sandy Koufax, one of baseball's greatest pitchers and the Cy Young Award winner in 1963, 1965, and 1966, in a collar ad for Manhattan Shirts. (*American Jewish Archives, Cincinnati*)

In the Baseball Hall of Fame are Hank Greenberg, the slugging star of the Detroit Tigers, and Sandy Koufax of the Los Angeles Dodgers, one of the finest left-handed pitchers the game has ever known, both Jewish. Benny Friedman of Michigan, Marshall Goldberg of Pittsburgh, and Sid Luckman of Columbia were renowned American football players. Luckman, the first great T-formation quarterback in professional football, made the Chicago Bears the dominant team of the National Football League in the 1940s, leading them to four NFL and five division championships. Nat Holman, an outstanding basketball player and coach from the 1920s to the 1960s, was among the first in a long line of basketball players from New York City. Perhaps the greatest swimmer of

his time is Mark Spitz, winner of seven gold medals in the 1972 Olympic Games and a California-bred Jewish American.

Albert A. Michelson, whose story has already been told in this book, was the first American to win a Nobel Prize in science. Brilliant other American scientists of Jewish origin followed in his footsteps: Felix Bloch, who measured nuclear magnetic moments; Melvin Calvin, who established the chemical reactions that occur during photosynthesis; Richard Feynman, well known for his work in high-energy physics; Murray Gell-Mann, for his research on the behavior of quarks, or subatomic particles; Donald Glaser, who designed a bubble chamber for the tracking of subatomic particles; Robert Hofstadter, for his work on the

Hank Greenberg, the star
first baseman of the
Detroit Tigers, who had a
lifetime batting average of
.313 with 331 home runs.
(*UPI*)

Sid Luckman, a superquarterback for the Chicago Bears, was elected to the Football Hall of Fame in 1965. (*Wide World Photos*)

linear accelerator and his studies of atomic nuclei; Isidor Isaac Rabi, for his research in nuclear physics, quantum mechanics, and magnetism; Julian Schwinger, for the advancement of knowledge in the field of quantum electrodynamics; E. G. Segrè, who discovered the antiproton; and other creative physicists and chemists, such as the Nobel laureates Leon Cooper, Burton Richter, William Stein, and Eugene Paul Wigner.

Isidor Isaac Rabi, the Nobel Prize winner, was brought to America as an infant and in 1937 became a professor of physics at Columbia. During the Second World War Rabi played a key role in the development of the atomic bomb and, along with J. Robert Oppenheimer, may be considered a pioneer in the field of nuclear weaponry. Oppenheimer, a Harvard-bred, Jewish American physicist, was director of the Los Alamos project and the so-called father of the atomic bomb. In later life both Rabi and Oppenheimer came to regard nuclear weapons as an abomination.

Norbert Wiener, the prodigy son of Leo Wiener, a philologist who wrote an important history of Yiddish literature in English, was the founder of cybernetics, whence came the computer and electronic calculator. Norbert Wiener, a glittering mathematician, was a professor at MIT for years.

Frank Schlesinger, born in New York and educated at City College, was an astronomer and director of the Yale University Observatory from 1920 to 1941.

Dr. J. Robert Oppenheimer, director of the Los Alamos project, which gave America the atom bomb, in the mid 1940s. (*UPI*)

Dr. Isidor Isaac Rabi, the Nobel laureate, at a Senate hearing in 1958; Rabi, one of the makers of the atom bomb, came to regard nuclear weapons as an abomination. (*Wide World Photos*)

Dr. Joseph Goldberger, for years the chief of the U.S. Public Health Service; Goldberger discovered the cause of and cure for pellagra in the 1910s. (*American Jewish Archives, Cincinnati*)

Julius Stieglitz, another Jewish American scientist, was president of the American Chemical Society, head of the chemistry department of the University of Chicago, and the brother of Alfred Stieglitz, one of America's greatest photographers.

The name of Emile Berliner, the inventor of the microphone and gramophone, rounds out this modest list of Jewish American scientists.

In the fields of physiology and medicine, American Jews have made and continue to make very impressive contributions. The tradition of reverence for the art of healing, which Jews brought with them to America in colonial times, goes back for more than 1,000 years; in medieval Europe, many Jewish scholars, philosophers, and poets were also physicians.

Samuel Nunez and Abraham de Lyon of Savannah, Isaac Hays of Philadelphia, and Si-

Dr. Judith Resnik of
Akron, Ohio, America's
first Jewish astronaut.
(*NASA*)

mon Baruch of South Carolina were leading Jewish physicians in early America. Of a later period were Jesse Lazear of Johns Hopkins, who gave his life in the fight against yellow fever; Joseph Goldberger, for years the head of the U.S. Public Health Service and the researcher who found the cause of and cure for pellagra, a crippling nutritional disease common among the Southern poor; Jacques Loeb, chief of the division of general physiology at the Rockefeller Institute for Medical Research; Simon Flexner, for years the director of laboratories at the Rockefeller Institute for Medical Research and a pioneer in the treatment of cerebrospinal meningitis; Milton Rosenau of Harvard, who founded the world's first school of public health there in 1909; Casimir Funk, one of the world's greatest biochemists, who was the discoverer of vitamins; and Abraham Jacobi, a renowned

lecturer on pediatrics and professor of children's diseases at New York Medical College, where in 1860 he opened the first children's clinic in the country.

Jonas Salk, who studied medicine at New York University, was born in New York City, the son of a garment worker. One of the nation's most celebrated medical researchers, Salk developed the vaccine that effectively ended the threat of dreaded poliomyelitis. He is the founder of the Salk Institute in La Jolla, California, where research is conducted into many other virus-related diseases. Albert Sabin, another graduate of New York University's medical school, is famous for his studies in virology and for the development of an alternate antipolio vaccine.

Among the many Americans of Jewish origin who were awarded the Nobel Prize in phys-

Dr. Abraham Jacobi, the renowned
American pediatrician, in 1910.
(*American Jewish Archives, Cincinnati*)

iology and medicine are Julius Axelrod, for
research into enzyme and hormone metabolism;
David Baltimore, for work on tumor viruses;
Konrad Bloch, for the metabolism of choles-
terol; Baruch Blumberg, the medical anthropol-
ogist who discovered the so-called Australian
antigen; Gerald Edelman, a pioneer researcher
in the field of immunology; Joseph Erlanger and
Herbert Gasser, for work on neurological trans-
missions; Arthur Kornberg, Joshua Lederberg,
and Marshall Nirenberg in genetics; and Fritz
Lipmann, Salvador Luria, Max Delbruck, Howard Temin, and George Wald.

Two of the many Nobel laureates deserve
special attention. Rosalyn Yalow, born in the
Bronx, was graduated from Hunter College and
began work as a secretary in 1941 at Columbia's
College of Physicians and Surgeons, where she

Dr. Jonas Salk, one of America's most
celebrated medical researchers, lecturing
on antivirus vaccines in 1980. (*UPI*)

Dr. Selman Waksman, the Nobel laureate who discovered antibiotics, at work in his laboratory in the 1950s. (*American Jewish Archives, Cincinnati*)

was permitted to take courses. After years of effort Dr. Yalow became associated with the Veterans Hospital in the Bronx and came to be its chief of nuclear medicine. In her original research she devised a comprehensive biochemical test to determine body changes from normalcy to disease. In 1977 Dr. Yalow was awarded the Nobel Prize in medicine, one of very few women so honored.

Selman Waksman, an immigrant Russian youth, arrived in America in 1910. His brilliance brought him to the attention of authorities at Rutgers University, where he was granted a degree in 1915. Three years later the University of California awarded him a Ph.D. in microbiology. At the New Jersey State Agricultural Experiment Station, where Waksman did most of his research, the immigrant scientist discovered antibiotics, the wonder "mycin" drugs that have saved countless lives the world over. Dr. Waksman donated more than 90 percent of the royalties he received from pharmaceutical companies to a research foundation at Rutgers State University.

PILGRIMS, PATRIOTS, settlers, adventurers, and immigrants, Jews came to these shores from the earliest times, and nowhere else have they become more thoroughly interwoven with the life, institutions, culture, and spirit of the pluralistic nation of which they form a vital part.

Millions of Jews, both past and present, have responded eagerly to the opportunities which, notwithstanding rebuffs and hostility from some quarters, democratic America offered them, and in their turn they have helped make this country a great nation.

Queen Victoria, it is said, once inquired of her prime minister Benjamin Disraeli what he felt was the most convincing evidence for the existence of God. Disraeli thoughtfully replied, "The Jews, Your Majesty." It is a miracle, perhaps greater than any biblical miracle, that the Jews, despite the worst kinds of vicissitudes, have survived for 5,000 years.